Summer Bridge™
EXPLORATIONS

K-1

CARSON-DELLOSA™
PUBLISHING GROUP

Greensboro, NC 27425 USA

Caution: Exercise activities may require adult supervision. Before beginning any exercise activity, consult a physician. Written parental permission is suggested for those using this book in group situations. Children should always warm up prior to beginning any exercise activity and should stop immediately if they feel any discomfort during exercise.

Caution: Before beginning any food activity, ask parents' permission and inquire about the child's food allergies and religious or other food restrictions.

Caution: Nature activities may require adult supervision. Before beginning any nature activity, ask parents' permission and inquire about the child's plant and animal allergies. Remind the child not to touch plants or animals during the activity without adult supervision.

The authors and publisher are not responsible or liable for any injury that may result from performing the exercises or activities in this book.

Summer Bridge™
An imprint of Carson-Dellosa Publishing LLC
PO Box 35665
Greensboro, NC 27425 USA
carsondellosa.com

Printed in the USA • All rights reserved.   ISBN 978-1-4838-1314-1

01-117151151

Table of Contents

Table of Contents (continued)

About Summer Bridge™ Explorations

Summer Bridge™ Explorations includes a variety of resources to prevent learning loss and keep your child thinking, doing, and creating throughout the summer. Practice pages review skills your child learned in kindergarten and preview first grade skills. Throughout, you'll find instructions for completing real-world explorations that encourage your child to actively explore the outdoors, use imagination, and apply skills. Find these resources inside:

- **Three sections that correspond to the three months of a traditional summer vacation**
  Each section begins with an introduction that describes the monthly theme and explains the two real-world explorations your child can choose to complete.

- **Real-world explorations**
  Six hands-on projects connect real-life learning with summer fun. Your child will keep learning alive by applying new skills as he explores the world, close to home and on the road. Look for these symbols beside step-by-step instructions for completing each exploration.

   Shapes in the Wild    Counting Book

   Travel Log    Animal Tracker

   ABC Book of Summer Adventures  Summer Fun Puppet Show

- **Learning activity pages**
  Age-appropriate activities include phonics, writing, counting, addition and subtraction, telling time, learning about shapes, and more. Activities become progressively more challenging as the summer continues. Each month, help your child choose practice pages to build skills and support explorations.

- **Character development and fitness activities**
  Throughout each section, quick activities offer fun ways to think about values, exercise the body, and build strength and fitness inside and out.

- **Bonus science, social studies, outdoor learning, and extension activities**
  These fun and creative activities are found in each section. Encourage your child to complete them as time allows.

- **Answer key**
  An answer key at the back of the book helps your child check her work.

Fitness and Character Development

Throughout *Summer Bridge™ Explorations*, you and your child will find fun and easy ways to build strong character and a healthy body. These activities encourage your child to think about values and to get fit by focusing on three essential components.

Flexibility

Using and stretching the muscles and joints regularly allows us to accomplish everyday tasks easily, like bending to tie a shoe. Challenge your child to set a stretching goal for the summer, such as practicing daily until he can touch his toes.

It is also important to be mentally flexible. Talk with your child about how disappointing it can be when things don't go your way. Explain that by being flexible, we can choose how we react to circumstances and "make lemonade" when life gives us lemons. Respecting the differences of others, sharing, and taking turns are all ways for your child to practice mental flexibility.

Strength

Your child may think that only people who can lift heavy weights are strong. Explain to your child that she is strong, too. Point out how much stronger she has become since she was a toddler. Many summer activities build strength, such as carrying luggage, riding a bike, swimming, and playing outdoor games.

Inner strength allows us to stand up for what we believe, even when others do not agree. Your child can develop this important character trait by being honest, helping others, and putting her best efforts into every task.

Endurance

Aerobic exercise strengthens the heart and helps blood cells deliver oxygen to the body more efficiently. This summer, limit screen time for your child and encourage him to build endurance by jumping rope, playing tag, hiking, or playing basketball.

Having mental endurance means sticking with something, even if it is difficult. Look for times when your child is growing frustrated or bored with an activity this summer. He may be reluctant to continue swim lessons, baseball practice, or reading a longer book. Whatever it is, encourage him to stay with the task in order to reap the rewards.

Index of Skills

Encouraging Summer Reading

Literacy is the single most important skill that your child needs to be successful in school. The following list includes ideas for ways that you can help your child discover the great adventures of reading!

- Establish a time for reading each day. Ask your child about what she is reading. Try to relate the material to a summer event or to another book.

- Let your child see you reading for enjoyment. Talk about the great things that you discover when you read.

- Choose books from the reading list (pages ix–x), or head to the library and explore. To select a book, have your child read a page aloud. If he does not know more than five of the words, the book may be too difficult.

- Read newspaper and magazine articles, recipes, menus, maps, and street signs on a daily basis to show your child the importance of reading informational texts.

- After you read a fiction book, ask your child to describe the main character to you. How does he or she look or behave? Present your child with several situations. Have her act out how the character would react to those situations.

- Choose several different types of books from the reading list. Talk about genres of books, like folktales, fairy tales, biographies, historical fiction, and informational texts. How many examples can you find from the reading list? Ask your child if he has a favorite type of book. Have your child paint a picture or create a collage that illustrates a book from his favorite genre.

- Make up stories or retell familiar stories. This is especially fun to do in the car, on camping trips, or while waiting at the airport. You can also have your child start a story and let other family members build on it.

- Find the author and illustrator names on the cover of a book and talk about what authors and illustrators do. Ask your child to use the illustrations to tell you about the story.

- Choose a nonfiction book from the reading list or the library. Before you begin reading, ask your child a question about the text. When you finish the book, ask her to write the answer to your question on a piece of paper. If she likes, she can add a drawing to illustrate it.

Summer Reading List

The summer reading list includes fiction and nonfiction titles. Experts recommend that parents read to kindergarten and first-grade children for at least 10 to 15 minutes each day. Then, ask questions about the story to reinforce comprehension.

Fiction

Allard, Harry
Miss Nelson Is Missing!

Banks, Kate
Max's Words

Beaty, Andrea
Rosie Revere, Engineer

Berger, Carin
The Little Yellow Leaf

Brett, Jan
Goldilocks and the Three Bears

Carle, Eric
The Mixed-Up Chameleon
The Very Quiet Cricket

Demi
The Empty Pot

Falconer, Ian
Olivia

Fleischman, Paul
The Matchbox Diary

Fleming, Candace
Papa's Mechanical Fish

Giganti, Paul, Jr.
Each Orange Had 8 Slices

Harris, Jim
Three Little Dinosaurs

Henkes, Kevin
Chrysanthemum

Hoberman, Mary Ann
A House Is a House for Me

Krauss, Ruth
The Carrot Seed

Miller, Pat Zietlow
Sophie's Squash

Priceman, Marjorie
How to Make an Apple Pie and See the World

Rylant, Cynthia
Night in the Country

Seuss, Dr.
The Shape of Me and Other Stuff

Silverstein, Shel
A Giraffe and a Half

Summer Reading List (continued)

Fiction (continued)

Slobodkina, Esphyr
Caps for Sale

Soto, Gary
Neighborhood Odes

Waber, Bernard
Ira Sleeps Over

Walsh, Ellen Stoll
Mouse Paint

Whybrow, Ian
Harry and the Bucketful of Dinosaurs
(formerly *Sammy and the Dinosaurs*)

Willems, Mo
Don't Let the Pigeon Stay Up Late!
Knuffle Bunny: A Cautionary Tale

Yolen, Jane
How Do Dinosaurs Say Goodnight?

Nonfiction

Bany-Winters, Lisa
*On Stage: Theater Games and Activities
    for Kids*

Bryant, Jen
*A Splash of Red: The Life and Art of
    Horace Pippin*

Burns, Marilyn
The Greedy Triangle

D'Angelo, Gus
San Francisco ABCs

Ehlert, Lois
Waiting for Wings

Gerstein, Mordicai
The Man Who Walked Between the Towers

Gray, Samantha
Eye Wonder: Birds

Hoban, Tana
Shapes, Shapes, Shapes

Huber, Raymond
Flight of the Honeybee

Jenkins, Steve and Robin Page
What Do You Do with a Tail Like This?

Lauber, Patricia
Be a Friend to Trees

Martin, Jacqueline Briggs
Snowflake Bentley

McCloud, Carol
*Have You Filled a Bucket Today?: A Guide
    to Daily Happiness for Kids*

Musgrove, Margaret
Ashanti to Zulu: African Traditions

Schwartz, David M.
If You Hopped Like a Frog

Stone, Tanya Lee
*Who Says Women Can't Be Doctors? The
    Story of Elizabeth Blackwell*

x

Section I Introduction

Theme: Learning in the Neighborhood

This month's explorations can be done close to home. They encourage your child to pay special attention to her surroundings and to notice new details about everyday places. Summer, with its more relaxed pace, is a great time for your child to explore the world nearby. Whether searching for insects in the yard or at the park, attending a farmers' market or community festival, or taking a walk around the block, you will find many opportunities to help your child observe and learn.

To build language arts and literacy skills this month, ask your child to find letters and words all around—on street signs, ads for yard sales and other events, and products at the store. Encourage her to name alphabet letters and the sounds they make and to use phonics skills to read words. To practice writing skills, your child may like to write a neighborhood newsletter, prepare menus for a special picnic or barbeque, or create directions for a new game to play outside with friends.

To build math skills this month, look all around for ways to count and use numbers. Let your child select and weigh a certain number of fruits at the market, count out coins to pay for an ice cream cone, or keep score during a family game. While exploring nature, encourage your child to notice the number of legs on an insect, the symmetry of leaves, or how many birds at a feeder belong to the same species.

Explorations

This month, your child will have a choice of two explorations. He may choose to follow steps for one or both. Review the explorations below with your child and help him make a choice. Emphasize that it is useful to have a path in mind from the start. Then, help your child find and complete the project activities according to his plan. Throughout the section, your child will see the icons shown below on pages that include directions directly related to one of the explorations. Emphasize that breaking a large project into smaller steps helps make it fun and easy to do.

0-20 Counting Book

With this exploration, your child will develop math and writing skills by finding groups of things in the neighborhood to count and record. They may be steps on a porch, kids at a picnic table, or tomatoes growing on a plant. For each group your child finds to count, he will take a photograph or make a drawing. The counting collection will lead to opportunities to tally and graph. Finally, your child will write a counting book to share his knowledge about numbers.

For young children, the skill of counting can be more challenging than adults may realize. Children must learn that, when counting, each number name should be assigned to only one object. The final number names the count of the entire group and stays the same no matter how objects in the group are arranged or rearranged. Have fun counting with your child this month. See how high he can count while jumping rope, collecting rocks or other small objects, or keeping track of sidewalk squares during a walk. If your child is ready, you may also introduce counting by twos and by tens.

Shapes in the Wild

With this exploration, your child will develop beginning math and geometry skills by cutting out and decorating 2-D shapes and then spotting those shapes out in the world. Your child will record each shape found by taking a photograph or drawing a picture. The collection of shapes will lead to opportunities for counting and graphing. Finally, your child will create a collage or photo album to share her knowledge about shapes.

It can be challenging for young children to identify shapes in the real world. 2-D shapes are usually part of 3-D figures, so you may need to guide your child to look at one surface, or face, of an object. Shapes in nature may be harder to spot because they will not likely be precise. Encourage your child to note approximate shapes as well as exact ones. You might talk about how something is almost a circle or very close to a square. If your child is ready, you may also discuss how squares are a type of rectangle as well as a type of rhombus.

Learning Activities

Practice pages for this month review skills your child learned in kindergarten. They also focus on skills that support the explorations described above. Preview the activities and choose several that target skills your child needs to practice. Also select several relating to the exploration(s) your child plans to complete. You may wish to mark those pages with a star or other symbol to let your child know to begin with those. Then, let your child choose practice activities that interest her and allow her to demonstrate her growing skills.

Counting Book, Step I

Numbers are everywhere! In this exploration, you will pay attention to the numbers of things that are all around you. For example, you might notice three trees in a row, six kids at a table, or 10 ducks in a pond. At the end of the month, you will turn what you saw into a counting book!

To begin, decide how high to count. Will your counting book go to 10, 15, or 20? Then, pay attention to your surroundings while you explore this month. As you find numbers of items, take pictures or make drawings of them. If it's easier, focus on one or two numbers each day. Use these two pages to keep track of the numbers of items you see as you explore. Write a brief description of each.

How many?	What did you see?
1	
2	
3	
4	
5	
6	
7	
8	

Counting Book, Step I (continued)

How many?	What did you see?
9	
10	
11	
12	
13	
14	
15	
16	
17	
18	
19	
20	

Write B or b to complete each word.

 Ball oy ook

ball oy ook

Say the name of each picture. Circle the pictures that begin with the /b/ sound, like ball.

FACTOID: Butterflies taste with their feet!

Trace and write the numbers 0, 1, 2, 3, 4, 5, and 6.

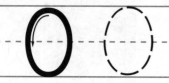

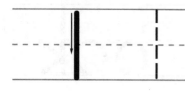

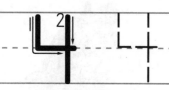

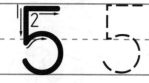

Write C or c to complete each word.

Car   an   at

car   an   at

Say the name of each picture. Circle the pictures that begin with the /c/ sound, like car.

Color each circle red. Color each square blue. Color each triangle yellow. Color each rectangle green.

Listen Up!

Being a good listener is part of being a good friend. But, listening is more than just hearing. Listening means paying close attention to what someone says.

Practice being a good listener. Ask a friend to describe a favorite activity. Pay close attention to what he or she says. Then, try to repeat what your friend said, but in your own words. If you don't understand your friend's description, ask a question that will help make it clear.

Shapes in the Wild, Step 1

Objects in real life are made up of shapes! In this exploration, you will search for shapes out in the world. You might see a tree made of triangles or a car with circles for wheels. Whatever shapes you notice, you will take or draw pictures of them. Then, at the end of the month, you will use those pictures to make a shape collage!

To prepare for your shape search, cut out a square, rectangle, triangle, rhombus, circle, and oval. Use the traceable shapes on this page and the next, or make larger shapes using a ruler and traceable objects in your home. Then, decorate each shape however you would like.

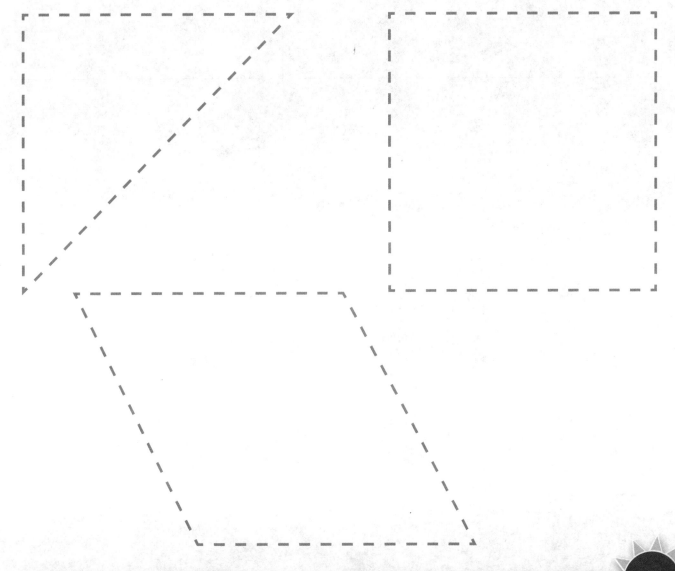

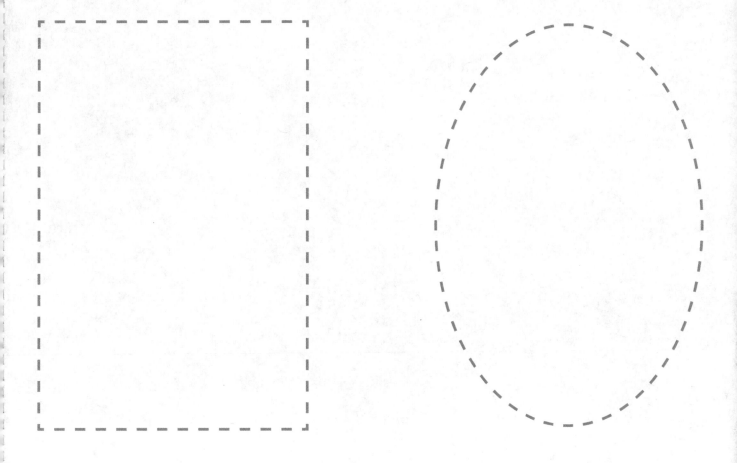

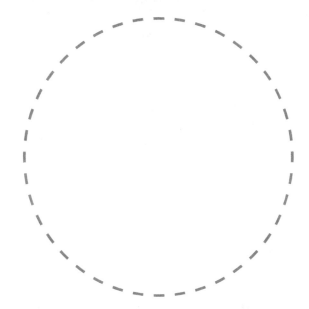

Write D or d to complete each word.

Door   og   esk

door   og   esk

Say the name of each picture. Circle the pictures that begin with the /d/ sound, like dog.

FACTOID: Not all ducks quack. Some grunt, squeal, or even whistle!

Trace and write the numbers 7, 8, 9, 10, 11, 12, and 13.

7 7

8 8

9 9

10 10

11 11

12 12

13 13

Write F or f to complete each word.

Fish   an   ox

fish   an   ox

Say the name of each picture. Circle the pictures that begin with the /f/ sound, like fish.

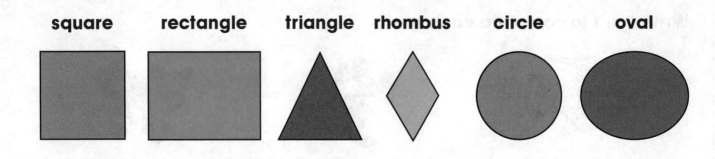

| square | rectangle | triangle | rhombus | circle | oval |

Color the shapes to match the shapes at the top of the page.

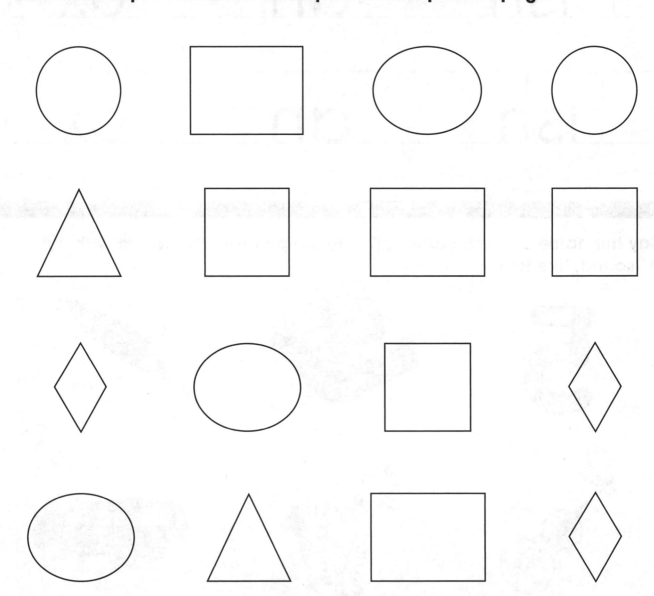

Write G or g to complete each word.

  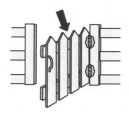

Gum   oat   ate

gum   oat   ate

Say the name of each picture. Circle the pictures that begin with the /g/ sound, like gum.

 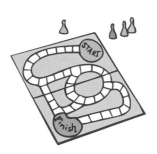 

FACTOID: Guitar strings are so strong that they can be used to cut chocolate.

Shapes in the Wild, Step 2

When you are out and about, look for squares, rectangles, triangles, rhombuses, circles, and ovals. If you can, carry your decorated shapes with you in a folder or notebook. When you see a shape in real life, take a picture of it or draw it, and include the matching decorated shape in each picture. Keep track of the shapes you find on the sheet below.

Shape	Where did you find the shape? Was it part of something else?
☐	
▭	
△	
◇	
○	
⬭	

Active Numbers

Play on your own or with a friend.

Write the numbers 1–10 on separate strips of paper. Fold the strips and place them in a hat or bag.

Draw a number from the hat. Say the number out loud. Then, choose an activity to do that number of times.

Each time you draw a number, pair it with a different activity so that every number goes along with just one activity. For example, you might hop 2 times, take 6 steps, and skip for 9 seconds.

Possible actions:

- Hops
- Skips
- Jumps
- Steps
- Lunges
- Stomps
- Arm circles
- Hand waves
- Claps
- Head nods

For an added challenge, try to remember the action that goes with each of your numbers. Then, when you run out of numbers, go through all of your numbered actions one after the other.

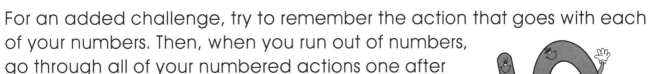

Night Walking

A cat's whiskers help it feel its way around at night!

A cat can see better than a human at night, as long as there's a little light. But, if it's completely dark, a cat can use its whiskers to feel where things are.

The whiskers are so sensitive that they can sense changes in the movement of air. For example, if a cat walks through the living room, it knows where furniture is because the air moves differently around large objects like couches.

How do you find your way in the dark? Do you shuffle your feet? Do you put your arms out and feel? Do you listen? Do you use your memory?

With an adult to help you, put on a blindfold and try to find your way around a room. Notice what sense you use the most. Try different strategies and keep track of how well they work.

Write H or h to complete each word.

Hand   at   am

hand   at   am

Say the name of each picture. Circle the pictures that begin with the /h/ sound, like hand.

Count the number of objects in each set. Write the number on the line.

1.

_____

2.

_____

3.

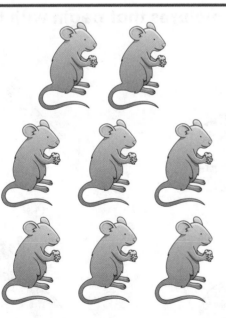

_____

4.

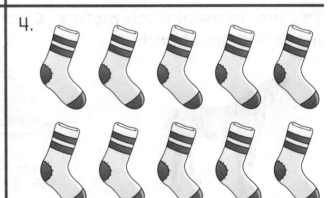

_____

Write J or j to complete each word.

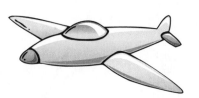  

Jet   ar   am

jet   ar   am

Say the name of each picture. Circle the pictures that begin with the /j/ sound, like jet.

 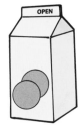 

FITNESS FLASH: Squat and hop like a frog 10 times.

23

Complete each shape to match the first shape in each row.

1.

2.

3.

4.

Write K or k to complete each word.

Kite ey ing

Kite ey ing

Say the name of each picture. Circle the pictures that begin with the /k/ sound, like kite.

Trace and write the numbers 14, 15, 16, 17, 18, 19, and 20.

14 14

15 15

16 16

17 17

18 18

19 19

20 20

Write L or l to complete each word.

Leaf   amp   ion

leaf   amp   ion

Say the name of each picture. Circle the pictures that begin with the /l/ sound, like leaf.

FITNESS FLASH: Bend over and touch your toes. Hold for 30 seconds.

Follow the directions in each row.

1. Color the circles red.	
2. Color the squares blue.	
3. Color the triangles green.	
4. Color the rectangles orange.	
5. Color the rhombuses purple.	
6. Color the ovals pink.	

CHARACTER CHECK: Show others that you care about what they have to say. When a friend is telling you something, try picturing it in your mind.

Write M or m to complete each word.

 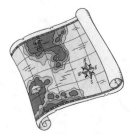 

Moon   ap   op

moon   ap   op

Say the name of each picture. Circle the pictures that begin with the /m/ sound, like moon.

Connect the dots from 1 to 10. Then, color to finish the picture.

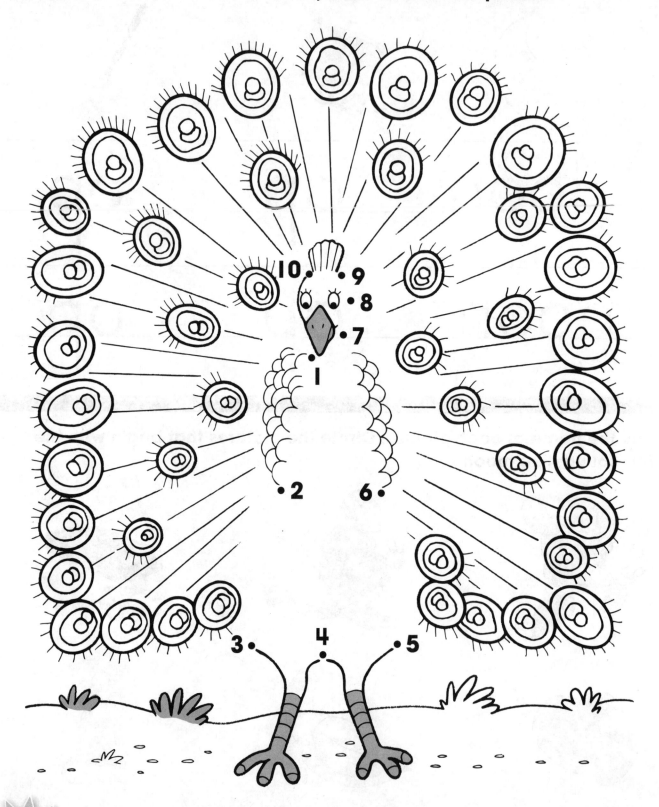

Take It Outside!

Nature is full of color! Trees, plants, grass, sky, animals, and insects help make up the rainbow of colors we see every day. Go outside with an adult and see how many different colors you can find in nature. You might even look for different shades of the same color. When you've found all the colors you can, draw a picture of the object you enjoyed looking at the most.

With an adult, use sidewalk chalk to write the alphabet. Then, for each vowel, draw a picture of something that begins with that letter.

Read the scavenger hunt list. Go outside with an adult. Try to find one object that matches each description.

Scavenger Hunt List

- something tiny
- something scratchy
- something smooth
- something pointy
- something pretty

- something round
- something soft
- something yellow
- something that opens
- something that smells good

BONUS

It's Only Natural!

Look at each object. Write M if the object is made by people. Write N if the object is natural (not made by people).

1.
   _____

2.
   _____

3.
   _____

4.
   _____

5.
   _____

6.
   _____

7.
   _____

8.
   _____

9.
   _____

10.
    _____

Write N or n to complete each word.

Nine   est   uts

nine   est   uts

Say the name of each picture. Circle the pictures that begin with the /n/ sound, like nine.

FITNESS FLASH: Do 5 karate kicks with each leg.

Write the name of each shape. Then, draw the shape.

 triangle

 _____

 _____

 _____

 REMINDER: How many shapes have you found so far? Which ones do you still need to find? Keep in mind that shapes in real life may not be perfect. If it looks close enough, use it!

Write P or p to complete each word.

Pie   ig   ark

pie   ig   ark

Say the name of each picture. Circle the pictures that begin with the /p/ sound, like pie.

Help the babies find their mothers. Then, color the pictures.

Write Q or q to complete each word.

Quilt   ueen   uail

quilt   ueen   uail

Say the name of each picture. Circle the pictures that begin with the /q/ sound, like quilt.

  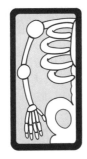

  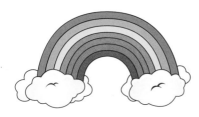

> **FACTOID:** A queen bee can lay over 2,000 eggs per day!

Draw the correct number of shapes in each box.

1.

2.

6 circles

4 rhombuses

3.

4.

5 triangles

9 ovals

Write R or r to complete each word.

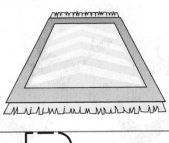  

Rug   ing   ain

rug   ing   ain

Say the name of each picture. Circle the pictures that begin with the /r/ sound, like rug.

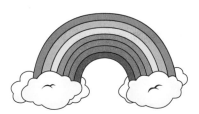  

  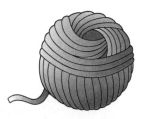

Put a counter (such as a penny) on each bird. Count aloud starting with 1.

1.

Write the numbers 1–10. Each number is 1 more than the one before.

2. _____

_____

_____

Write the next two numbers.

3. _____   _____

- - - - - - - - - - -   - - - - - - - - - - -

2, 3 _____   7, 8 _____

0-20 **REMINDER:** Have you looked for numbers of items for your counting book this week? Anytime you go for a walk or go someplace new, try to bring a camera or a pencil and paper with you to capture what you see.

Write S or s to complete each word.

Soap   aw   ock

soap   aw   ock

Say the name of each picture. Circle the pictures that begin with the /s/ sound, like soap.

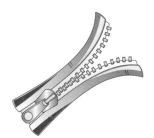  

FACTOID: Fur seals can use their hind feet to walk.

Draw the shape that comes next in each pattern. Color the shapes.

1.

2.

3.

4.

Start Your Day Right!

Eating a healthy breakfast helps you have energy all day, and that energy will help you stay fit. Try this fun and delicious recipe!

Breakfast Parfait

$\frac{1}{4}$ cup granola

$\frac{1}{2}$ cup plain yogurt

$\frac{1}{4}$ cup berries or chopped fruit

1 TBS maple syrup

In a parfait glass or a tall cup, layer ingredients. Start with the granola, then add the yogurt, the fruit, and finally the maple syrup. Enjoy!

No-Blow Balloons!

Follow these steps and watch your balloon fill up like magic!

Materials
- baking soda
- vinegar
- 16-oz. plastic bottle
- 2 funnels
- a balloon

Procedure

Step 1: Get help from an adult.

Step 2: Use one funnel to fill the plastic bottle about $\frac{1}{3}$ full with vinegar.

Step 3: Stretch your balloon so that it can be blown up easily.

Step 4: Use the other funnel to fill the balloon about halfway with baking soda.

Step 5: Fit the balloon opening over the bottle opening and make a good seal. Be careful not to spill any baking soda into the bottle just yet.

Step 6: Hold the balloon opening against the bottle top to keep it in place. Then, tip the balloon so that the baking soda falls into the bottle.

Step 7: Keep holding the bottle top as the mixture fizzes, releasing the gas that blows up your balloon!

BONUS

Communication Today

Look at the hand-written letter. In the past, if people wanted to keep in touch, they had to write and mail letters. Draw one faster way we use to communicate today.

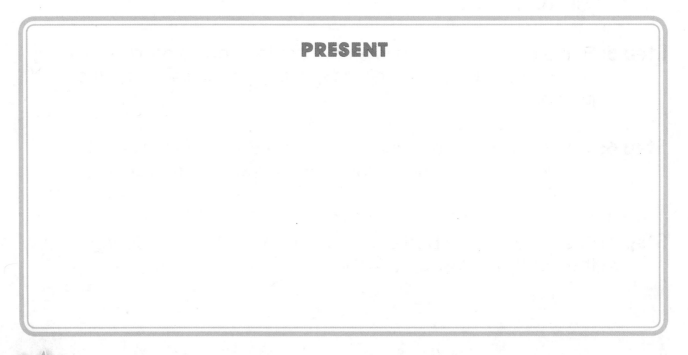

Write T or t to complete each word.

Top	ent	iger
top	ent	iger

Say the name of each picture. Circle the pictures that begin with the /t/ sound, like top.

Count the sets in each box. Color the set that has more.

1.

2.

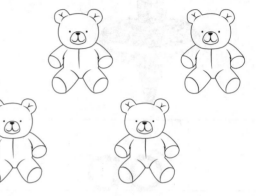

3.

4.

Write V or v to complete each word.

Van   ase   est

van   ase   est

Say the name of each picture. Circle the pictures that begin with the /v/ sound, like van.

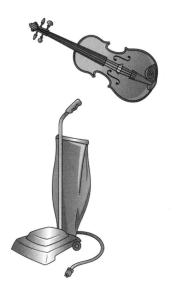

FITNESS FLASH: Crab walk across the room and back.

Draw the shape that comes next in each pattern. Color the shapes.

1.

2.

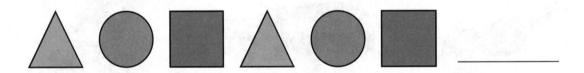

3.

4.

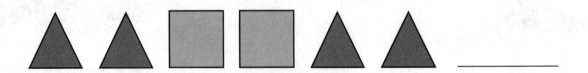

Write W or w to complete each word.

Wig   hale   eb

wig   hale   eb

Say the name of each picture. Circle the pictures that begin with the /w/ sound, like wig.

Count the objects in each set. Write the number on the line.

1.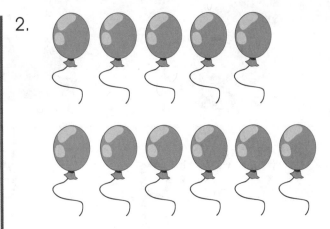

2.

_____

3.

_____

4.

_____

Write X or x to complete each word.

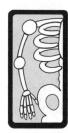 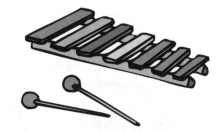

$\times$-ray   ylophone

$\times$-ray   ylophone

Say the name of each picture. Circle the pictures that begin or end with the /ks/ sound, like X-ray or box.

FACTOID: Foxes have whiskers on their legs as well as their faces.

Circle the car that comes next in each row.

1.

2.

3.

4.

Write Y or y to complete each word.

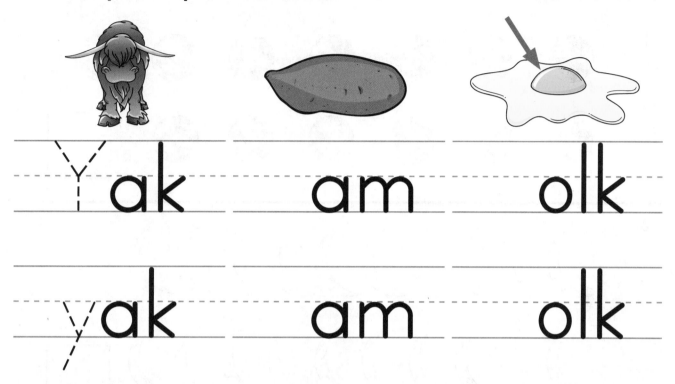

Yak   am   olk

yak   am   olk

Say the name of each picture. Circle the pictures that begin with the /y/ sound, like yak.

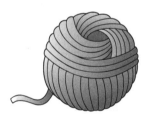

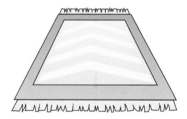

Count the objects in each set and write the number in the box.

1.

2.

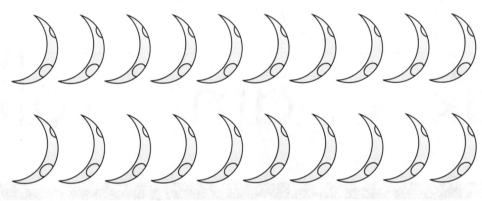

Complete the second picture to match the first picture in each set.

3.

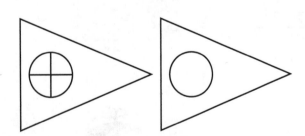

4.

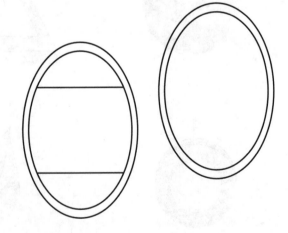

Counting Book, Step 2

Were you able to find all the numbers you were looking for? If not, now is the time to fill in the gaps. Use your imagination to draw the missing numbers of items. If you want, your whole book could come from your imagination. It's up to you!

Are any numbers missing?   **yes   no**

If so, which numbers? _____

Draw pictures for each number you're missing. Use the space below to sketch ideas.

Counting Book, Step 2

Before getting started on your counting book, there are some things you should think about. For example, will the numbers in your book go up or down? Will you include the number 0? Will you do something special on the page that has your favorite number?

Fill out the planner below to get ready to create your book!

1. My book will begin with the number _____.

2. My book will end with the number _____.

3. My favorite number is _____.

4. On the page with my favorite number, I will _____

_____.

5. My book will be made up of

   a. all photos
   b. all drawings
   c. both photos and drawings

6. Here are some title ideas for my book:

_____

_____

_____

7. Here are some pictures I could draw on the front cover:

Community Helpers

Look at each picture. Draw a line to match each community helper to the correct tool.

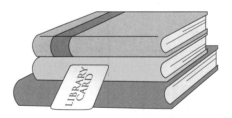

Family Cooperation Journal

People in a family cooperate to get things done. Each day, talk about something you accomplished together. In the spaces below, write about what you did. Let each person who helped sign his or her own name.

	What We Did	Who Helped
Monday		
Tuesday		
Wednesday		
Thursday		
Friday		

Write Z or z to complete each word.

Zoo   ip   ero

zoo   ip   ero

Say the name of each picture. Circle the pictures that begin with the /z/ sound, like zoo.

FACTOID: You can tell how a zebra is feeling by the way its ears are pointing.

Circle the plate with more apples.

1.

Circle the bowl with fewer fish.

2.

CHARACTER CHECK: Think about a time when a friend shared with you. How did it make you feel?

Practice writing uppercase and lowercase As.

Write a to complete each word.

c t   nt   h m

Say the name of each picture. Circle the pictures that have the short a sound, like cat.

Fill in the missing uppercase letters on the lines.

A, B, ___, ___, E, ___,

___, H, ___, ___, ___,

___, M, ___, ___, ___,

Q, ___, S, ___, ___,

___, W, ___, ___, Z

CHARACTER CHECK: Why is it important to tell the truth? Can you think of a time when it is better not to be honest?

Practice writing uppercase and lowercase Es.

E E   e e

Write e to complete each word.

g g   p   n   b   l l

Say the name of each picture. Circle the pictures that have the short e sound, like egg.

FITNESS FLASH: Stand on one foot and stretch your arms up like tree branches. Hold for 20 seconds and then switch legs.

63

Ms. Harper's class made this graph showing their favorite animals. Study the graph and answer the questions.

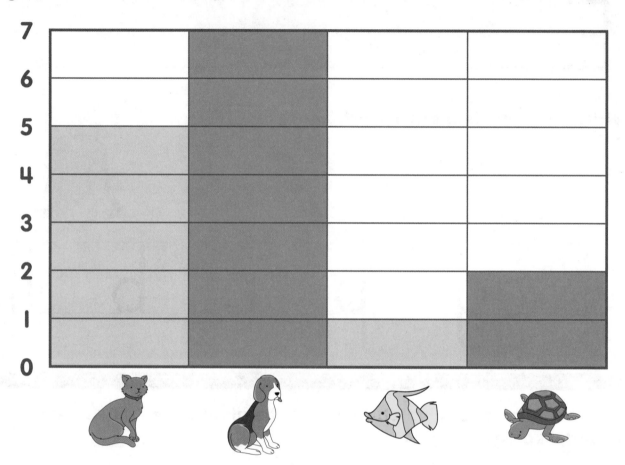

1. How many students like cats best? _____

2. How many students like dogs best? _____

3. How many students like fish best? _____

4. How many students like turtles best? _____

Practice writing uppercase and lowercase Is.

Write i to complete each word.

 b   b   f  sh m  lk

Say the name of each picture. Circle the pictures that have the short i sound, like bib.

Fill in the missing lowercase letters on the lines.

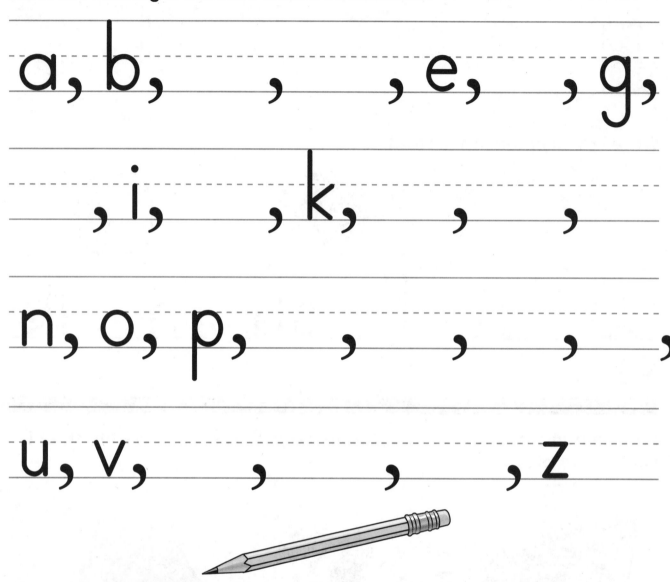

a, b, ___ , ___ , e, ___ , g,

___ , i, ___ , k, ___ , ___ ,

n, o, p, ___ , ___ , ___ , ___ ,

u, v, ___ , ___ , ___ , z

Take Responsibility

A responsibility is something people count on you to do. Think of it like a job. Responsibilities you may have are doing your homework, brushing your teeth, and cleaning your room. What is one responsibility of yours? On a separate sheet of paper, draw a picture to show what would happen if it didn't get done.

Practice writing uppercase and lowercase Os.

O O o o

Write o to complete each word.

fr___g   l___ck   d___ll

Say the name of each picture. Circle the pictures that have the short o sound, like frog.

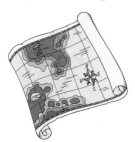  

FACTOID: The smallest species of frog is not even as wide as a penny.

Practice writing uppercase and lowercase Us.

Write u to complete each word.

   p   s   n   d   ck

c p s n d ck

Say the name of each picture. Circle the pictures that have the short u sound, like cup.

Counting Book, Final Step

You are ready to make your counting book! Follow the directions below.

Materials

- your pictures and drawings of counted items (It's okay to include made-up things, too.)
- paper large enough to hold your pictures and still have room for words (You will use both sides of each sheet, so if you have 20 pictures, you will need 10 sheets of paper plus 2 for your cover.)
- glue or tape
- markers, colored pencils, or crayons
- stapler

Directions

1. Put your pictures in order. If a picture needs to be drawn and colored again, do that. Then, make any final tweaks.

2. Decide what to write at the top of each page. Each page should include at least the number and name of the items in your picture (example: 12 Black Birds).

3. Write the words that go on each page, making sure to leave enough room for the picture.

4. Glue or tape your pictures to their matching pages.

5. Make a front and back cover for your book. Be sure to include the title and author (That's you!) on the front cover.

6. Ask an adult to staple your book together.

0-20

Counting Book

Finished Product Examples

You can be creative with your book. Think about what would make your book the most fun to write. Here are some examples to think about:

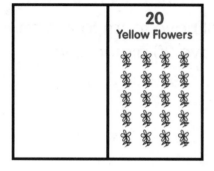

In this book, the numbers go down, all the way to 0. The author chose a favorite thing to have zero of—chocolate cake.

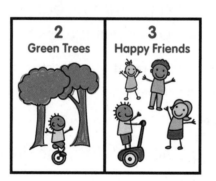

In this book, the author included himself on each page, walking, riding, or driving by. As the numbers increase, his way of getting around becomes more powerful.

Shapes in the Wild, Final Step

You are ready to make your shape collage! Follow the directions below.

Materials

- your pictures of shapes in the wild
- your decorated shapes
- poster board
- construction paper
- scissors
- pictures
- glue
- markers (optional)

Directions

1. Cut out shapes of different colors and sizes from construction paper.

2. Place your shape pictures, decorated shapes, and cut-out shapes on the poster board. Try out different ways to arrange your shapes. You might like to try one of these ways:
   - all of one shape clustered together
   - mixed shapes arranged by color
   - different shapes put together to look like objects
   - shapes in random order, however they look good to you

3. Use markers to write any words you would like to include on your poster. Maybe you want to title your collage or write the names of the shapes.

4. Once you are happy with how everything fits together on the poster board, glue down the shapes. This step takes patience and can get messy. Try using as little glue as possible.

5. Show off your work!

Shapes in the Wild

Finished Product Examples

Your collage can look any way you want. Here are examples of different arrangements on the page:

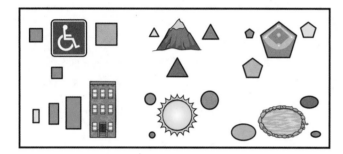

This collage is arranged by shape.

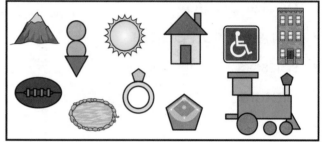

This collage is arranged so that shapes come together to look like objects.

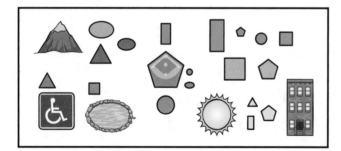

This collage is arranged by color.

This collage is in random order.

Then and Now

Look at the pictures. Circle each picture that shows something from the present. Draw an X on each picture that shows something from the past.

Is Seeing Believing?

A horse cannot see what's directly in front of its face. That's because a horse's eyes are located on the sides of its face. So, when something is right in front of its forehead, the horse can't see it. This is called a *blind spot*.

Did you know humans have blind spots, too? We don't realize it because our brains fill in the missing details for us. Say you're looking at an apple tree, and one part of an apple is in your blind spot. Instead of showing you a black spot where your blind spot is, your brain will fill in that spot to match the apple around it. Pretty cool, huh?

Try this activity to find your blind spot!

Step One: Hold this page in front of you, and close your right eye.

Step Two: Look at the X below. You should also be able to see the dot, but only out of the corner of your eye. Remember, only your left eye is open.

Step Three: Now, move the page slowly away from you, keeping your eye focused on the X. In one particular spot, the dot will seem to disappear. That's your blind spot!

Step Four: See if the same thing happens when you move the paper up and down or side to side. What happens if you make the dot bigger? What if you turn the page upside down?

X

Section II Introduction

Theme: Travel and Learn

This month's explorations can be completed while traveling to places near and far. They encourage your child to build knowledge and make connections while visiting new and familiar places. Engage your child in family travel plans by looking at maps together, choosing destinations and activities, and reflecting on cultural experiences. Whether you travel to a family reunion, to a state or national park, or to another part of the world, you will find many opportunities to help your child learn during your adventures.

To build language arts and literacy skills this month, invite your child to help you use guidebooks, brochures, and websites to research travel destinations. Long car rides and waits at the airport are perfect opportunities to read books, tell stories, and play word games together. During your trip, purchase postcards and encourage your child to use them for writing simple messages to friends and relatives back home.

To build math skills this month, point out to your child the important role that numbers play when traveling. Mile markers, gallons of gasoline purchased, hours traveled, time zone changes, and admission prices to attractions all make great real-world math lessons. Use situations from your travel adventures to invent simple addition and subtraction word problems for your child to solve. During road trips, notice numbers on license plates of passing vehicles and use them for more math practice.

Explorations

This month, your child will have a choice of two explorations. He may choose to follow steps for one or both. Review the explorations below with your child and help him make a choice. Emphasize that it is useful to have a path in mind from the start. Then, help your child find and complete the project activities according to his plan. Throughout the section, your child will see the icons shown below on pages that include directions directly related to one of the explorations. Emphasize that breaking a large project into smaller steps helps make it fun and easy to do.

 Travel Log

With this exploration, your child will develop graphing, writing, and organizational skills by keeping track of places visited during the month and noticing details about them. Trips may be short (to the local library, shopping mall, or park) or long (to another town, state, or country). Your child will take note of special features and details about each place. The notes she takes will provide opportunities for counting, graphing, and organizing information. Finally, she will create a travel ad that encourages others to visit a favorite place.

Organizing and categorizing information is a critical thinking skill that becomes easier with practice. When thinking about places your child visits this month, have fun categorizing information in different ways. On index cards, draw or paste pictures or write a few words to describe each place. Then, sort the cards in different ways. Which places are inside? Which are outside? Which are fun to visit? Can your child put the cards in order from nearest to your home to farthest?

 Animal Tracker

With this exploration, your child will develop science and writing skills by observing wildlife during summer adventures. He will keep track of animals he sees close to home and far away. For each type of animal, your child will write a simple description, take a photograph, or make a drawing. The collection of animals will lead to opportunities for counting, graphing, and research about animal traits. Finally, your child will create a guidebook to share what he has learned about animals and attempt to act out each animal's behavior for family members to guess.

As your child describes animals, encourage him to use all of his senses. How does an earthworm feel? How does a duck look? How does a chipmunk sound? How does a pig smell? Begin with verbal descriptions that include lots of sensory details and move on to written descriptions. Emphasize that good writers capture all the details of an experience. Search your child's picture books to find and read aloud examples of vivid descriptions.

Learning Activities

Practice pages for this month move from kindergarten review to an introduction of first grade skills. They also focus on skills that support the explorations described above. Preview the activities and choose several that target skills your child needs to practice. Also select several relating to the exploration(s) your child plans to complete. You may wish to mark those pages with a star or other symbol to let your child know to begin with those. Then, let your child choose practice activities that interest her and allow her to demonstrate her growing skills.

Travel Log, Step I

You can find something exciting almost anywhere you go! In this exploration, you will keep track of the places you go. Then, at the end of the month, you will make an ad for your favorite place!

Use this sheet to track where you go. You may want to include parks, libraries, friends' and relatives' houses, restaurants, or even supermarkets. Put a tally mark in the "Number of Times" column each time you visit a particular place. Then, write down a highlight (something you really liked) about each place. Continue on a separate sheet of paper, if needed.

Place Visited	Number of Times	Highlights

Animal Tracker, Step I

Learn about animals just by observing them! In this exploration, you will look and listen for animals wherever you go. When you see a new animal, you will take or draw a picture of it and write a short description. Then, at the end of the month, you will use your findings to make a guidebook about animals!

Use this sheet to keep track of the animals you see and hear this month. Look for animals in your yard, in the neighborhood, in nearby parks, or wherever your travels take you. Take pictures or draw the animals you see. Then, write the animal's name, where it was found, what it was doing, and any sounds it made. Continue on a separate sheet of paper, if needed. If you don't know the name of the animal, your picture should help you find out.

Animal	Where Found	Animal's Actions and Sounds

Say the name of each picture. Write a to complete each word that has the short a sound heard in cat.

1.

____ nt

2.

f ____ n

3.

t ____ p

4.

m ____ p

5.

c ____ t

6.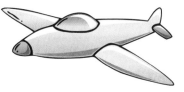

j ____ t

79

Color the spaces on the umbrella. Use the number key to help you.

1   3   5   7 = yellow
2   4   6   8 = purple

Imagine what it's like to be someone in the picture. Describe something you see, hear, smell, taste, and touch. Use words that show what you picture in your mind.

EXAMPLE: I see <u>brightly colored balloons</u>.

1. I see _____ .

2. I hear _____ .

3. I smell _____ .

4. I taste _____ .

5. I touch _____ .

Add to find each sum.

1. 3 + 1 = _____

2. 4 + 1 = _____

3. 3 + 0 = _____

4. 2 + 2 = _____

5. 1 + 3 = _____

6. 5 + 0 = _____

7. 1 + 4 = _____

8. 2 + 3 = _____

9. 1 + 1 = _____

Say each word. Listen for the short a sound. Draw an X on the words that do not have the short a sound.

cap

ant   pig

sad   bed

make   can

had   tag

FACTOID: The first baseball hats were made out of straw.

Look at the pictures below. Draw a line to match each picture to its opposite.

Connect each set of shapes as shown to make a new shape. Circle the new shape.

1. 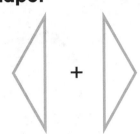 +  =

2.  + =

Complete the other half of the picture.

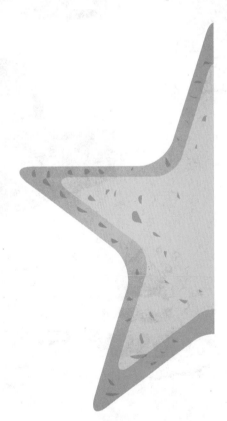

Write the next number in each set.

1.

| 5 | 6 | |

2.

| 2 | 3 | |

3.

| 17 | 18 | |

Read each sentence aloud. Listen for the short a sound. Circle each word that has the short a sound.

4. The cat ran and sat.

5. The sad rat jumped high.

6. Seth has a blue hat.

7. The man has two maps.

CHARACTER CHECK: Do something to help a friend or family member today.

Color each picture the correct color.

red shirt

yellow ball

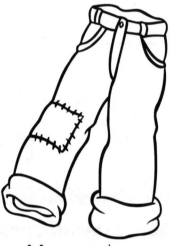

blue pants

green car

Trace and write each letter.

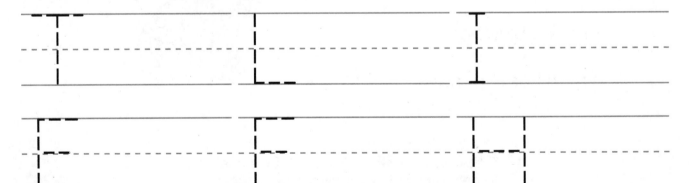

Add to find each sum. Place beans on the jar below to help you solve the problems.

1. 6
    + 1

2. 8
    + 2

3. 5
    + 4

4. 3
    + 6

5. 9
    + 1

6. 7
    + 3

7. 5
    + 3

8. 4
    + 2

Take Charge of Your Learning!

Make a list of things you want to know more about. Write down what you already know about each topic. Then, write what else you would like to find out.

The next time you're at the library, check out a book or magazine that will help you learn what you want to know.

Read the poem. Underline all the words that have the short a sound. Then, answer the questions.

Imagine That!

What would you say
to a bat in a hat
if he asked you to play
in a stack made of hay?

What if the plan
was to skate with a cat
by the lake where the man
with the fan gets a tan?

Would you hop in a cab?
Catch a train with your dad?
Or be glad to be asked?
Grab a snack! Have a blast!

1. What event from the poem does the picture show?
   a. skating with a cat
   b. playing in a haystack
   c. catching a train

2. Which way to leave is not named in the poem?
   a. catching a train
   b. taking a cab
   c. riding a bus

FACTOID: The inventor of roller skates crashed into a mirror the first time he wore them in public.

Declare Your Independence!

On the Fourth of July, we celebrate our country's independence. One way the U.S. shows its independence is by flying the nation's flag. The stars, stripes, and colors represent our 50 states, the 13 original colonies, and the things that are important to our country.

Now, celebrate your own independence by designing a flag that represents you! Consider what shapes and colors show your personality, your unique family, or maybe just your favorite things. You decide!

If It Quacks Like a Duck

Not all ducks quack. Some grunt, squeal, or even whistle!

The words we use to describe animal sounds cannot ever truly sound like the animals. In fact, many of the words we use for animal sounds are not very accurate. Try this activity to find out what animals actually "say."

With an adult, listen to animals in your neighborhood, in the park, at the zoo, at a fair, or on a farm.

After listening closely, try to make the sound each animal truly makes. Maybe you heard several dogs barking. Did they all sound the same?

How would you spell the sounds you heard? Write them down on a sheet of paper.

How different is each real sound from the sound word associated with that animal?

Say the name of each picture. Write e to complete each word that has the short e sound heard in egg.

1.

b __ ll

2.

t __ nt

3.

h __ n

4.

v __ st

5.

t __ n

6.

b __ b

On each number line, draw a dot on the first even number. Then, skip count by 2s. Draw a dot on each even number in the pattern. The first pattern has been started for you.

1.

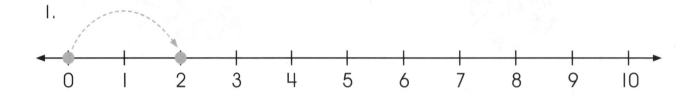

2.

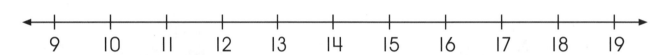

Now, skip count by 10s. Draw a dot on each multiple of 10. The pattern has been started for you.

3.

FITNESS FLASH: Hop on one leg 10 times. Then, switch legs.

Writing an Opinion

When you write about your opinion, your goal should be to persuade others to think what you think. In order to get your audience to agree with you, you have to provide reasons for the way you feel.

Practice providing reasons for your opinion. First, think of a game that you really like to play. Use the graphic organizer below to give four reasons for liking that game. Follow the example.

EXAMPLE

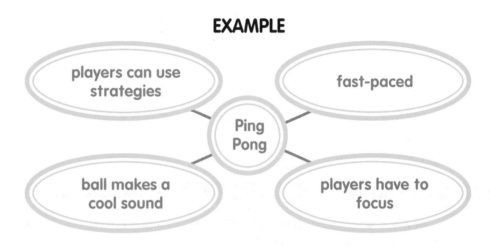

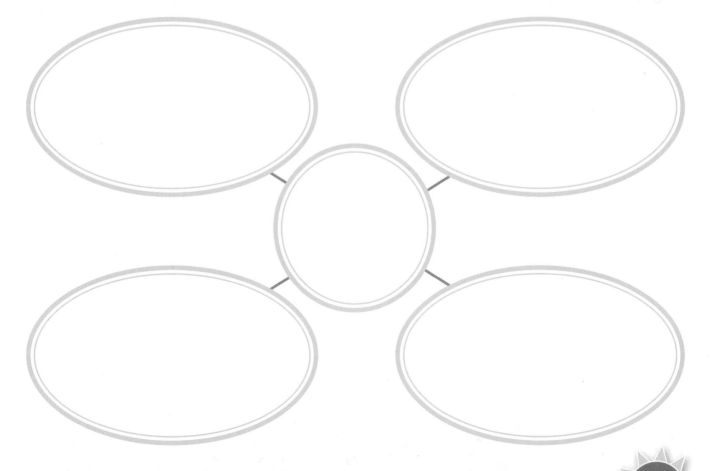

Subtract to find each difference.

1. 3 – 1 = _____

2. 3 – 2 = _____

3. 4 – 2 = _____

4. 4 – 1 = _____

5. 5 – 4 = _____

6. 5 – 3 = _____

7. 2 – 1 = _____

8. 4 – 3 = _____

9. 4 – 0 = _____

Say each word. Listen for the short e sound. Draw an X on the words that do not have the short e sound.

bed

pet   ten

meet   jet

bag   net

web   team

FACTOID: Not all spiders spin webs.

Circle the three objects that most belong together in each row.

Divide each rectangle into two triangles. Color one triangle blue and the other triangle yellow.

Complete the other half of the picture.

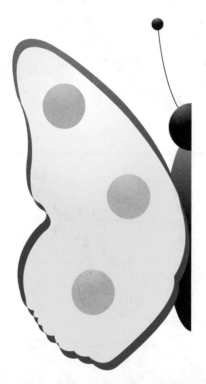

Write the first number in each set.

1.  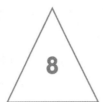 8  9

2.   14  15

3.  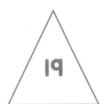 19  20

Read each sentence aloud. Listen for the short e sound. Circle each word that has the short e sound.

4. Jed is in his bed.

5. Peg has a pet hen.

6. Ben and Wes have five toy jets.

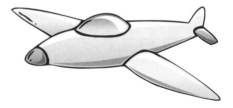

7. Beth has a red pen.

FITNESS FLASH: Do 10 push-ups.

Color each picture the correct color.

orange block

pink pig

purple balloon

brown bear

Trace and write each letter.

Subtract to find each difference. Place beans on the jar below to help you solve the problems.

1. $\begin{array}{r} 6 \\ -1 \\ \hline \end{array}$ 2. $\begin{array}{r} 9 \\ -2 \\ \hline \end{array}$

3. $\begin{array}{r} 8 \\ -3 \\ \hline \end{array}$ 4. $\begin{array}{r} 7 \\ -4 \\ \hline \end{array}$

5. $\begin{array}{r} 10 \\ -5 \\ \hline \end{array}$ 6. $\begin{array}{r} 10 \\ -7 \\ \hline \end{array}$

7. $\begin{array}{r} 6 \\ -4 \\ \hline \end{array}$ 8. $\begin{array}{r} 9 \\ -6 \\ \hline \end{array}$

Your Happy Place

Draw the place that makes you feel the happiest. Maybe it's your best friend's house, the city pool, or your backyard. Draw yourself in that place doing what you like to do best. Include in the picture the friends and family you would most like to have with you. Give your picture a title.

Read the poem. Underline all the words that have the short e sound. Then, answer the questions.

Heading West

Ben dressed in red pants and a vest,
Packed his bags, and left for the West.
He knew it was time that he went
When a bird made a nest in his tent.

No, Ben did not feel so safe in his bed
With a bird hanging over his head.
So he jumped in his jeep with a yell,
And sped off to a new place to dwell*.

*dwell *v.* to live

1. What color are Ben's pants?
   a. blue
   b. black
   c. red

2. Why is Ben leaving?
   a. Ben does not like camping.
   b. A bird is in Ben's tent.
   c. Ben misses his family.

3. How is Ben getting to the West?
   a. in a jeep
   b. on an airplane
   c. on a bicycle

4. In the last line of the poem, what does "sped off" mean?
   a. jumped high
   b. went away fast
   c. dropped something

REMINDER: Have you looked for new animals this week? Anytime you go someplace where animals might be, try to bring a camera and pencil and paper with you. That way, you can record what the animal looks like and any sounds it makes.

Symbols on Maps

A symbol is a picture that stands for something that is shown on a map. Symbols used in a map are shown in the Map Key. Look at the symbols. Draw a line from each symbol to what it stands for in the drawing below.

Cornstarch Quicksand

What is quicksand?

Quicksand is a mixture of water and sand that sometimes acts like a liquid and other times acts like a solid. If you step into it slowly, it moves around like thick water. But, if you move quickly, it feels hard, like wet sand on the beach.

Most likely, you will never experience quicksand in real life. But, you can feel what it's like by making this simple mixture!

Materials

- large plastic mixing bowl
- 2 cups cornstarch
- I cup water
- spoon

Procedure

Step I: Make sure you have an adult to help you.

Step 2: Add $\frac{1}{2}$ cup of cornstarch to the mixing bowl.

Step 3: Slowly add $\frac{1}{4}$ cup of water to the cornstarch, stirring gently.

Step 4: Keep slowly adding cornstarch and water, stirring until all of the cornstarch and water are completely mixed together.

Step 5: Put your hand in the mixture and slowly move your fingers. Notice how it feels like a thick liquid.

Step 6: Sink your whole hand into the "quicksand." Now, grab a handful of the stuff and try to pull it up. This is what it feels like for your feet to sink in quicksand!

Step 7: Try knocking on the surface of the quicksand. Now, it should feel like a solid. The harder you hit it, the more solid it should feel. Cool, right?!

Step 8: To clean up, put your quicksand in a plastic bag and throw it into the trash. (It will clog the drain if you wash it down the sink.)

Say the name of each picture. Write i to complete each word that has the short i sound heard in fish.

1.

   w ___ g

2.

   s ___ x

3.

   s ___ n

4.

   w ___ b

5.

   p ___ n

6.

   sh ___ p

Make a pet chart. Ask 20 people if they have a pet.

Use tally marks to show what kind.

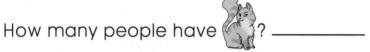				Other	None

Tally Marks
| = 1
|| = 2
||| = 3
|||| = 4
|||| = 5

Use your pet chart. Write the number.

How many people have 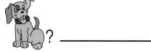? _____

How many people have ? _____

How many people have ? _____

How many people have ? _____

How many people do not have a pet? _____

How many people have a pet that is not on the chart? _____

Complete.

Which pet is the favorite? _____

Which pet is the least favorite? _____

CHARACTER CHECK: Sometimes, it is frustrating not to understand something. What can you do when you don't understand?

Imagine what it's like to be someone in the picture. Describe something you see, hear, smell, taste, and touch. Use words that show what you picture in your mind.

EXAMPLE: I hear <u>waves crashing on the sand</u>.

1. I see _____ .

2. I hear _____ .

3. I smell _____ .

4. I taste _____ .

5. I touch _____ .

Add or subtract to solve each problem.

1. 2
   + 3
   ____

2. 5
   − 1
   ____

3. 5
   + 0
   ____

4. 3
   − 0
   ____

5. 3
   + 1
   ____

6. 2
   − 1
   ____

7. 4
   + 1
   ____

8. 5
   − 5
   ____

9. 2
   + 2
   ____

10. 4
    − 2
    ____

Say each word. Listen for the short i sound. Draw an X on the words that do not have the short i sound.

fin

ride

hid

bug

win

in

it

sit

red

FACTOID: Most fish cannot swim backward.

The sentence below uses all letters of the alphabet. Use it to practice your handwriting.

The wizard's very big ox jumped quickly for change.

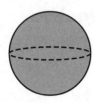   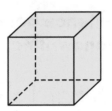

Color the shapes to match the shapes above.

 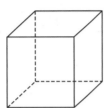 

 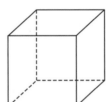 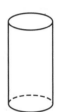

Circle the picture that shows the cat _over_ the dog.

Circle the picture that shows the truck _next to_ the toy box.

Add or subtract to solve each probem. Use the 10 dots below to help you solve.

1.	10 − 6	2.	9 − 9	3.	3 + 5	4.	5 + 1
5.	4 + 2	6.	10 − 5	7.	7 + 3	8.	10 − 8
9.	7 − 4	10.	6 + 4	11.	9 − 7	12.	2 + 5

Read each sentence aloud. Listen for the short i sound. Circle each word that has the short i sound.

13. Jim hid the bib in a bag.

14. The fish swim in the pond.

15. The big cat did a flip.

16. Jill had to fill the bucket Tim spilled.

FITNESS FLASH: Lie on your stomach, lift your arms and legs off the floor, and pretend to swim. Do this three times for 10 seconds each.

The sentence below uses all letters of the alphabet. Use it to practice your handwriting.

A dozen brave ex-knights will quest for juicy plums.

Touch each number in order. Say it aloud with an adult. Then, touch each multiple of 10. Say it aloud with an adult.

1	2	3	4	5	6	7	8	9	10
11	12	13	14	15	16	17	18	19	20
21	22	23	24	25	26	27	28	29	30
31	32	33	34	35	36	37	38	39	40
41	42	43	44	45	46	47	48	49	50
51	52	53	54	55	56	57	58	59	60
61	62	63	64	65	66	67	68	69	70
71	72	73	74	75	76	77	78	79	80
81	82	83	84	85	86	87	88	89	90
91	92	93	94	95	96	97	98	99	100

Read the poem. Underline all the words that have the short i sound. Then, answer the questions.

Big Hit

At the farm shindig*, there's a pig in a wig
Who is dancing a jig—I'm not lying.
Now, her twin starts to spin on the floor with a grin,
But she steps on a pin and goes flying.

In the air, she does flips as she snacks on some chips
That she had in her lips the whole time.
The first sis is in bliss* as she sees all of this.
See, her twin's found a new way to dine!

*shindig *n.* party
*bliss *n.* great happiness

1. How many pigs are talked about in the poem?
   a. two
   b. three
   c. four

2. What happens to make one of the pigs fly into the air?
   a. She snacks on some chips.
   b. She spins on the floor.
   c. She steps on a pin.

3. What is a jig?
   a. a kind of dance
   b. a kind of snack
   c. a kind of toy

FACTOID: Pigs are very smart, maybe even smarter than a three-year-old child.

City Streets

Every town has some interesting street names. Streets can get their names in many different ways. They are often named after presidents, states, trees, and flowers. What are some of the interesting street names in your town?

People's Names	Places	Funny Names
Numbers	Natural Features	Animals
Plants and Trees	Directions	Other

BONUS

Using sidewalk chalk, draw a pattern of circles, squares, rectangles, triangles, ovals, and rhombuses on the sidewalk. Jump from shape to shape, saying the shape's name as you land. See how fast you can go!

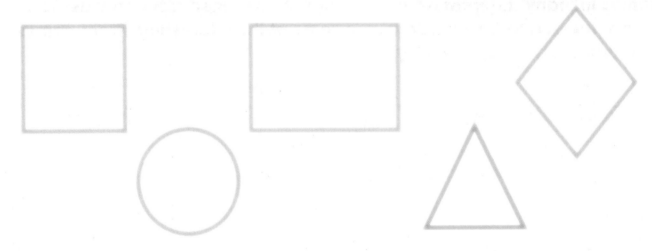

With an adult, investigate five different flowers in your neighborhood or park. Draw a picture of each and describe its smell.

Ask an adult to set up a "Simon Says" obstacle course with you. Find items you can safely go over, under, around, and through. Then, wait for Simon to say exactly how to get past each obstacle. For example, Simon might tell you to go "over the bucket" and "under the swing."

Say the name of each picture. Write o to complete each word that has the short o sound heard in frog.

1.

f ___ x

2.

cl ___ ck

3.

l ___ ck

4.

b ___ g

5.

v ___ n

6.

s ___ ck

Use the calendar to answer each question.

July

Sunday	Monday	Tuesday	Wednesday	Thursday	Friday	Saturday
		1	2	3	4	5
6	7	8	9	10	11	12
13	14	15	16	17	18	19
20	21	22	23	24	25	26
27	28	29	30	31		

1. What day of the week is July 14? _____

2. What day of the week is the first day of July? _____

3. What date is the second Wednesday? _____

4. What day of the week is July 31? _____

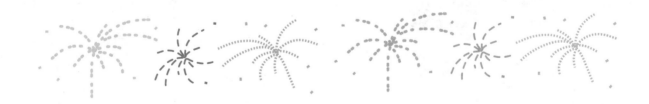

CHARACTER CHECK: What is one mistake you made recently? What did you learn from that mistake?

In each row, circle the three objects that most belong together.

Add or subtract to solve each probem. Use the 10 dots below to help you solve.

1. 10
   − 3

2. 9
   + 1

3. 2
   + 3

4. 4
   − 2

5. 9
   − 5

6. 3
   + 4

7. 5
   + 2

8. 10
   − 9

Say each word. Listen for the short o sound. Draw an X on the words that do not have the short o sound.

top

dog   root

rope   fog

box   got

stop   bib

FACTOID: Some insects drink droplets of fog!

Look at the picture below. Circle the things that go fast. Draw an X on each thing that is slow.

Look at the picture graph.

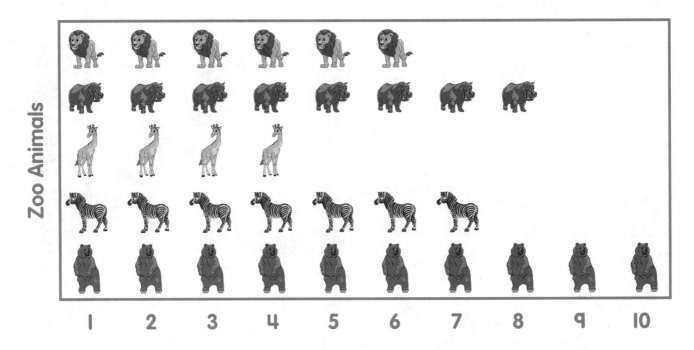

Circle the one that has more.

Circle the one that has fewer.

How many ![lion]? _____

How many ![hippo] ? _____

How many ![giraffe] ? _____

How many ![zebra] ? _____

How many ![bear] ? _____

Add or subtract to solve each problem.

1. 6 + 2 = _____   2. 5 – 1 = _____   3. 4 + 3 = _____

4. 8 – 1 = _____   5. 2 + 8 = _____   6. 9 – 0 = _____

7. 3 + 5 = _____   8. 10 – 6 = _____   9. 7 + 2 = _____

10. 9 – 8 = _____   11. 1 + 9 = _____   12. 6 – 3 = _____

Read each sentence aloud. Listen for the short o sound. Circle each word that has the short o sound.

13. The frog can hop on top of the box.

14. The dog and the fox ran to the pond.

15. John put the box by the rock.

16. Tom went for a jog.

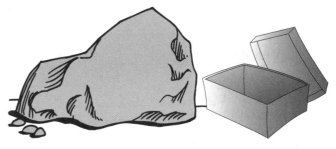

FITNESS FLASH: Bear-walk across the room and back.

Make a food chart for one day. Show what you ate.

Fruit	Vegetable	Meat/Eggs/Fish	Bread/Cereal	Other Foods

Breakfast	
Lunch	
Dinner	
Snacks	

Use your food chart.

1. How many of each did you eat?

   Fruit _____   Bread/Cereal _____

   Vegetable _____   Other Foods _____

   Meat/Eggs/Fish _____

2. What food did you eat the most? _____

3. At which meal did you eat the most? _____

4. What is your favorite food? _____

Follow the directions to draw a picture.

1. Draw 1  in the middle of the pig's face to make a nose.

2. Draw 2 ● inside the nose to finish it.

3. Draw 1 ◡ underneath the nose to make a mouth.

4. Draw 2 • above the nose to make eyes.

5. Draw 2 ▷ on either side of the head to make ears.

Read the poem. Underline all the words that have the short o sound. Then, answer the questions.

Fox on Ox

I am shocked by that fox!
He is riding an ox,
One that could not be any braver.

The fox trots past our tots,
Showing off what he's got—
An ice cream that's strawberry flavor!

He shares not a drop,
Doesn't slow down or stop
Till he's slurped the thing down, cone and all.

Then, he laughs as he hops
Up on top of a shop.
If he isn't more careful, he'll fall!

1. The speaker of the poem is shocked because
   a. a fox is shopping in town.
   b. an ox is being very brave.
   c. a fox is riding an ox.

2. What does the fox show off?
   a. his ox
   b. his ice cream
   c. his shop

3. What word best describes the fox?
   a. angry
   b. caring
   c. unsafe

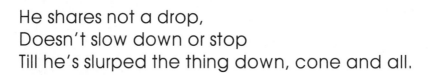

FITNESS FLASH: Lie on your back with your hands above your head. Stretch up through your fingers and down through your toes. Hold for 20 seconds.

124

Travel Log, Step 2

Make a picture graph to show how often you visited each place on your list this month. You'll need a different picture to represent each place. If you need help, follow the example on p. 120. Use the graphing frame below or create your own on a separate sheet of paper.

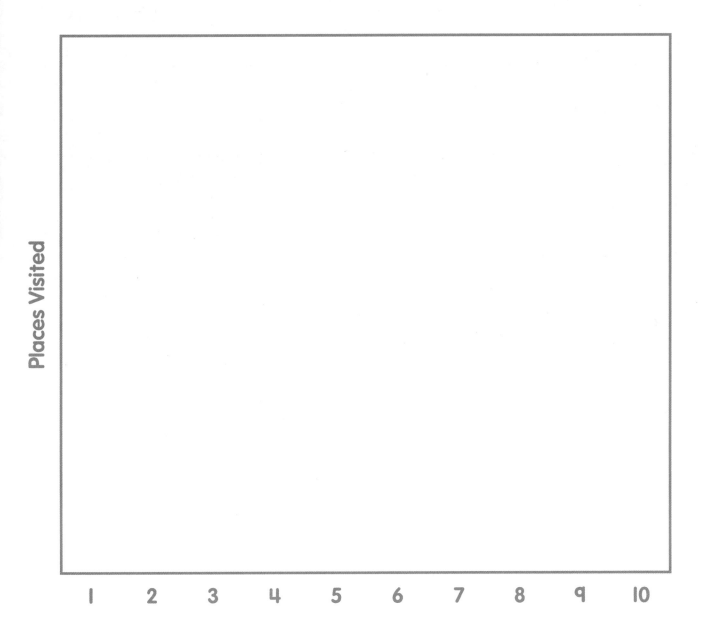

Places Visited

1   2   3   4   5   6   7   8   9   10

Animal Tracker, Step 2

Animal Tracker, Step 2

Now, add your own imaginary animal to the list. Draw and color it in the space below. Then, name your animal and say how it moves and what sound it makes.

Name of animal: _____

How it moves: _____

What sound it makes: _____

126

© Carson-Dellosa

Hummingbird Nest

A hummingbird's nest is no bigger than a ping-pong ball. Try making your own to understand just how tiny this bird's nest is!

Step 1: Ask an adult to help you. Find a ping-pong ball or a whole walnut in its shell to use as a mold. Your nest will be the size of one of these but cut in half.

Step 2: Make self-hardening clay from a recipe you find on the Internet, or tear off a piece of aluminum foil, about 4 inches long.

Step 3: Fold and shape the clay or foil to fit around half of the ping-pong ball. If you don't have a walnut or ping-pong ball, use the sphere below to decide how big to make your nest.

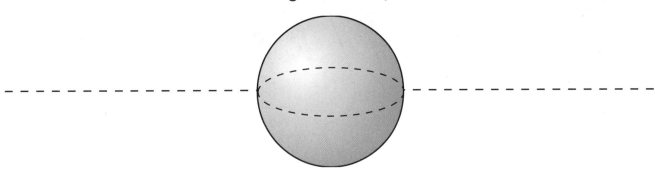

Step 4: Once you've built the nest (and waited for the clay to harden), find objects either in the house or outside that will fit in the nest. Maybe you can find some small objects to represent baby birds or bird eggs. How much can you fit in the nest? Is there anything you thought would fit that didn't?

Extra Step: What if you were as tiny as a hummingbird? How would the world look to you? How do you think humans would look to you? What about a leaf on a tree? A flower? Draw a picture of something through a hummingbird's eyes.

BONUS

Take a Hike

This is a map showing three hiking trails.

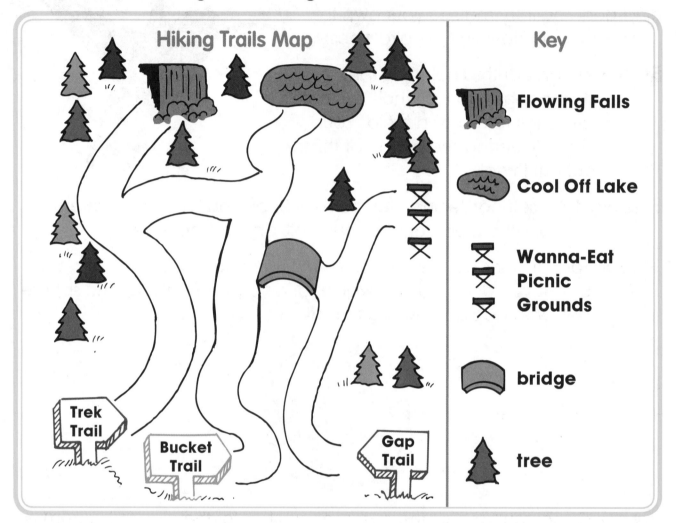

Directions

1. Draw a red line along the trail that leads to the Wanna-Eat Picnic Grounds.

2. Draw a yellow line along the trail that leads to Flowing Falls.

3. Draw a green line along the trail the leads to Cool Off Lake.

4. Draw a blue line to show how you can go from Trek Trail to Cool Off Lake.

5. Draw an orange line to show how you can go from Bucket Trail to the Wanna-Eat Picnic Grounds.

Say the name of each picture. Write u to complete each word that has the short u sound heard in cup.

1.

t___b

2.

p___g

3.

d___ck

4.

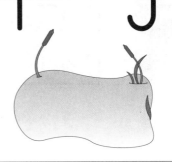

p___nd

5.

h___g

6.

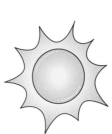

s___n

Circle all of the 2-D shapes. Mark an X over all of the 3-D shapes.

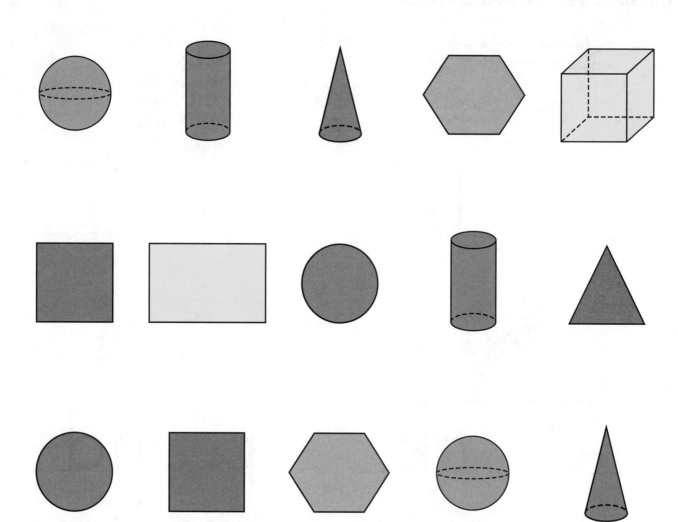

Dance Moves

Make up a dance to a song you like. Create moves for your legs, your arms, and your whole body. Dance to the beat of the song, and see if you can make up enough moves to last 16 beats. Once you have learned your dance by heart, teach it to a friend. Then, ask your friend to make up a dance to teach to you!

130

Follow the clues below. Circle your choices.

1. Find the object that is brown and hard.

2. Find the object that is yellow and long.

3. Find the object that is green and sour.

4. Find the object that is blue and tiny.

Write the missing numbers in each fact family.

1. Family: 2, 3, 5

   3 + ☐ = 5

   2 + 3 = ☐

   5 − ☐ = 2

   5 − 2 = ☐

2. Family: 3, 1, 4

   1 + ☐ = 4

   3 + 1 = ☐

   4 − 3 = ☐

   4 − ☐ = 1

Say each word. Listen for the short u sound. Draw an X on the words that do not have the short u sound.

rug

book   fun

dug   hat

cube   us

up   shut

FACTOID: Reading storybooks can make you better at understanding how other people feel.

Circle the picture that is most different in each row.

Follow the directions to draw a picture.

1. Draw 1 ● in the center of the page to make a body.

2. Draw 1 ● on top of the big circle to make a head.

3. Draw 8 ⋀ around the big circle to make legs.

4. Draw 2 ○ in the small circle to make eyes.

Write the missing numbers in each fact family.

1. Family: 3, 6, 9

    6 + ☐ = 9

    3 + 6 = ☐

    9 − ☐ = 3

    9 − 3 = ☐

2. Family: 2, 5, 7

    5 + ☐ = 7

    2 + 5 = ☐

    7 − 2 = ☐

    7 − ☐ = 5

Read each sentence aloud. Listen for the short u sound. Circle each word that has the short u sound.

3. The lucky duck swam on the pond.

4. Mom cut the bud off of the shrub.

5. Gus chewed gum on the bus.

6. Judd washed the mud out of the rug.

CHARACTER CHECK: Be brave and try something new this week.

Circle the numbers that match the first number in each row.

25	25	52	20	25	22	55	25	26
98	96	89	98	93	88	98	99	98
16	10	61	18	16	26	16	67	16

Color each word the correct color. Then, write the word on the line.

red

blue

yellow

green

Nouns can name things.

car

ball

Fill in the missing letters in the nouns that name things. Use the words in the box to help you.

chair   desk   book   apple   pen   bag

ba__   bo__k   ap__le

des__

pe__

__hair

Read the poem. Underline all the words that have the short u sound. Then, answer the questions.

Get Up, Pup!

Each day after lunch at about one o'clock
Chuck has little luck getting his pup to wake up.

He calls his pup's name and lets in the sun
But for that pup to get up, Chuck must beat a drum!

The pup does not like this—it is not at all fun—
He drags himself up, but his eyes are still shut!

So Chuck gives him a hug and a muffin with nuts.
The pup opens his eyes and, at last, he says, "Ruff!"

1. What problem does Chuck have?
   a. His pup is late for lunch.
   b. His pup will not wake up.
   c. His pup does not like drums.

2. How do we know when the pup is really awake?
   a. He beats a drum.
   b. He gets out of bed.
   c. He opens his eyes and barks.

3. Which sentence best describes Chuck?
   a. Chuck cares about his pup.
   b. Chuck is angry with his pup.
   c. Chuck wants his pup to play drums.

Travel Log, Final Step

On page 93, you practiced writing an opinion. When you write an advertisement, or ad, your goal is to get people to have a good opinion about whatever it is you're advertising. Since you chose for your ad a place you like to go, your goal here is to make other people want to go there, too.

Directions

1. Choose the place you liked best from your graph on page 125.
2. Fill in the worksheet below to get ready to write your ad.
3. Look at the example on page 140 to get writing ideas.
4. Write your own ad on a separate sheet of paper.
5. Perform your ad for an audience. Think about recording it so that you can play it like an ad on the radio.

What is the name of your chosen place? _____

What can people do there? _____

What did you like about it? _____

What do you think other people will like the most about this place?

_____

_____

What sound effects could you use in your ad? Start by thinking about what sounds you heard when you visited the place you're advertising.

_____

_____

Travel Log
Finished Product Example

Notice how the author of this ad gets the listeners' attention and then shows them what makes the library so great.

WAVERLY PUBLIC LIBRARY RADIO AD

Are you looking for an adventure this summer?

Pick up a book at the Waverly Public Library!

Imagine you're in Africa with monkeys, lions, and giraffes! [monkey and lion sounds] Pretend you were there when the first robot was made! [robot sounds] Solve a mystery like a detective! Make an imaginary friend!

Be anyone, anywhere with a book from the Waverly Public Library!

Come to the comfy couches in the kids' reading section! And, on Wednesdays, listen as Ms. Huffman reads some of her favorite picture books out loud. You can even grab a healthy snack at the snack bar!

You may not get to Africa this summer, but you can get to the Waverly Public Library! See you there!

This grabs the listeners' attention.

The author uses sound effects to make the ad more exciting.

The place name is repeated so people remember it.

The author included his three favorite things about the library.

Animal Tracker, Final Step

You are ready to make your animal guidebook! Follow the directions below.

Materials
- your pictures and drawings of animals, including your imaginary one
- your worksheet from page 78 and any additional sheets you used to track animals
- paper large enough to hold your pictures and still have room for words (You will use both sides of each sheet, so if you have 10 pictures, you will need 5 sheets of paper plus 2 for your cover.)
- glue or tape
- markers, colored pencils, or crayons
- stapler

Directions
1. Decide on an order for your pictures. You might organize animals by type or put them in ABC order. Don't forget to include your imaginary animal!
2. Put your pictures in order. If a picture needs to be drawn and colored again, do that. Then, make any final tweaks.
3. Decide how to lay out the pages of your book (see the examples on page 142). Each page should include the animal's name, its picture, the sound it makes, and what it was doing when you saw it.
4. Write the words that go on each page, making sure to leave enough room for the picture.
5. Glue or tape your pictures to their matching pages.
6. Make a front and back cover for your guidebook. Be sure to include the title and author (That's you!) on the front cover.
7. Ask an adult to staple your book together.

OPTIONAL: When you have finished your guidebook, use it to play a game with your friends and family. See if they can guess each animal's name based on what you say and do. Start by moving like the animal. Then, say where the animal was found. Finally, make the sound the animal makes. Include your imaginary animal just for fun!

Animal Tracker
Finished Product Examples

You can design your guidebook however you like. Here are some ways you could lay out your pages:

Squirrel	Robin
Sound: "Yab-dab-dab-dab-dab"  The squirrel was running up the trunk of a tree.	Sound: "Cheer, cha-ree, cheer up!" The robin was flying from branch to branch.

Squirrel	Robin

Sound: "Yab-dab-dab-dab-dab"	Sound: "Cheer, cha-ree, cheer up!"
Action: The squirrel was running up the trunk of a tree.	The robin was flying from branch to branch.

Squirrel		Robin	
Says, "Yab-dab-dab-dab-dab"	The squirrel was running up the trunk of a tree.	Says, "Cheer, cha-ree, cheer up!"	The robin was flying from branch to branch.

Weight-Lifting Ants

Did you know that an ant can lift 20 times its own weight? Try this experiment to see an ant in weight-lifting action!

Step 1: Find an anthill in your yard or in the park. Make sure you can see ants coming out of the hill. Since most ants are especially attracted to sweets, bring a small cookie, brownie, or a bit of cake with you.

Step 2: Step a foot or two away from the anthill and drop a small crumb of cookie. Wait and see if an ant picks it up.

Step 3: Keep trying bigger and bigger crumbs and pieces, waiting in between for an ant to take each one away.

Step 4: How big does the crumb need to be before an ant won't pick it up? Will another ant help, or will the piece just be left?

Step 5: Draw the crumb sizes as best you can and write your observations next to each one.

BONUS

Heroes

Who is your hero? Answer the questions. Draw a picture of this person in the box.

Name : _____

What do you like about this person?

_____

_____

_____

_____

What would you like to do with this person?

_____

_____

_____

_____

Section III Introduction

Theme: My Summer Adventures

This month's explorations invite your child to reflect on her experiences as the end of summer vacation approaches. They encourage her to use her growing skills to tell her own stories in imaginative ways. Before the beginning of a new school year, take the time to talk with your child about how much she has grown and changed. Measure and record her height and weight and look back at old photos together. Ask her to show off how good she is at swimming, playing sports, reading and writing words, doing math problems, and other skills that show her growing maturity. Make sure to ask what she is looking forward to learning in the new school year.

To build language arts and literacy skills this month, visit the library and challenge your child to choose a book that is a little longer or more difficult than what she is used to. Read the book to her several times, and then ask her to read it to you. Take advantage of back-to-school sales and purchase supplies for a home writing center. These can include pencils, pens, markers, envelopes, notebooks, index cards, and stickers. Encourage your child to write letters and stories for fun every day.

To build math skills this month, challenge your child to count as high as she can while jumping rope or bouncing a ball. Go on a search for two- and three-digit numbers around your home and read them together to build knowledge of place value to the tens place and hundreds place. Provide a ruler and ask her to measure toys. Which toy is tallest or longest? How much taller is she than the tallest toy?

Explorations

This month, your child will have a choice of two explorations. He may choose to follow steps for one or both. Review the explorations below with your child and help him make a choice. Emphasize that it is useful to have a path in mind from the start. Then, help your child find and complete the project activities according to his plan. Throughout the section, your child will see the icons shown below on pages that include directions directly related to one of the explorations. Emphasize that breaking a large project into smaller steps helps make it fun and easy to do.

ABC ABC Book of Summer Adventures

With this exploration, your child will develop language arts and writing skills by creating an alphabet book that chronicles summer experiences. She will think about summer experiences such as playing **t**ag, going to the **z**oo, or riding her **b**ike, using her imagination to find one that represents each letter of the alphabet. For each summer adventure, she will write a description and take a photograph or draw a picture. The collection of ideas will lead to opportunities to put words in alphabetical order. Finally, she will compile all the information to make an alphabet book to share.

To help your child complete this exploration, provide a print or online children's dictionary and children's thesaurus. Explore the resources together, noticing that they are organized alphabetically. Call out a few simple words and ask your child to locate them in the books or search for them using the search tool. Model how to use the thesaurus to find synonyms that may help her include all the letters of the alphabet in the ABC book. For example, synonyms for *walking* include *hiking*, *strolling*, and *trotting*.

Summer Fun Puppet Show

With this exploration, your child will develop language arts skills and fine motor skills by writing a play, making puppets, and performing a puppet show about his summer adventures. Your child will use household items to create puppets who will be the stars of the show. Then, he will think about favorite summer experiences and use them to write short scripts. Finally, he will act out the puppet show for family and friends.

Speaking, listening, and performance skills are important to school and personal success. Praise your child's growing ability to speak clearly and confidently. Have fun together using silly poems and tongue twisters to develop speaking skills. As your child rehearses his puppet show, model being a good listener. Encourage him to speak loudly and clearly during the performance. When show time arrives, make a video recording of the event. Watch the video together and congratulate your child on his success.

Learning Activities

Practice pages for this month introduce skills your child will learn in the first grade. They also focus on skills that support the explorations described above. Preview the activities and choose several that target skills your child needs to practice. Also select several relating to the exploration(s) your child plans to complete. You may wish to mark those pages with a star or other symbol to let your child know to begin with those. Then, let your child choose practice activities that interest her and allow her to demonstrate her growing skills.

ABC Book of Summer Adventures, Step 1

Do something fun for every letter of the alphabet! In this exploration, you will take or draw pictures of your summer adventures. Then, you will turn those adventures into an ABC book!

To begin, make a list of your favorite things to do in the summer. Maybe you like making popsicles with your parents, playing baseball with friends, or going swimming at the lake. Include any favorite things you have done so far plus anything you would like to do before you go back to school. Continue on a separate sheet of paper, if needed.

FAVORITE SUMMER ACTIVITIES

1. _____
2. _____
3. _____
4. _____
5. _____
6. _____
7. _____
8. _____
9. _____
10. _____
11. _____
12. _____

Summer Fun Puppet Show, Step I

Before going back to school, relive the summer! In this exploration, you will turn your favorite summer adventures into a puppet show!

To begin, think about all the fun things you have done this summer. Did you travel anywhere? Did you have a particularly fun day at the park? Did you sleep over at a friend's house? Make a list of your adventures. Is there anything else you would like to do before back-to-school? Put those on the list, too, and see if you can make them happen. Continue on a separate sheet of paper, if needed.

SUMMER ADVENTURES

1. _____
2. _____
3. _____
4. _____
5. _____
6. _____
7. _____
8. _____
9. _____
10. _____
11. _____
12. _____

Add to find each sum.

1. 6 + 2 = _____

2. 5 + 1 = _____

3. 4 + 3 = _____

4. 1 + 7 = _____

5. 2 + 8 = _____

6. 9 + 0 = _____

7. 3 + 5 = _____

8. 4 + 6 = _____

9. 7 + 2 = _____

Circle the first letter of each word below. Then, put the words in ABC order. The first one is done for you.

10.

ⓒar   ⓑird

___**bird**___

___**car**___

11.

moon   two

_____

_____

12.

nest   fan

_____

_____

13.

card   dog

_____

_____

14.

pig   bike

_____

_____

15.

sun   pie

_____

_____

Write the beginning sound for each picture.

1.

_____

- - - - - - - - -

_____

2.

_____

- - - - - - - - -

_____

3.

_____

- - - - - - - - -

_____

4.

_____

- - - - - - - - -

_____

5.

_____

- - - - - - - - -

_____

6.

_____

- - - - - - - - -

_____

7.

_____

- - - - - - - - -

_____

8.

_____

- - - - - - - - -

_____

9.

_____

- - - - - - - - -

_____

10.

_____

- - - - - - - - -

_____

11.

_____

- - - - - - - - -

_____

12.

_____

- - - - - - - - -

_____

Subtract to find each difference.

1. 6 – 2 = _____   2. 5 – 1 = _____   3. 7 – 3 = _____

4. 8 – 7 = _____   5. 10 – 8 = _____   6. 9 – 0 = _____

7. 8 – 4 = _____   8. 10 – 6 = _____   9. 7 – 2 = _____

10. 9 – 1 = _____   11. 6 – 3 = _____   12. 10 – 4 = _____

Put each row of words in ABC order. If the first letters of two words are the same, look at the second or third letters.

13. __1__ candy   __2__ carrot   __4__ duck   __3__ dance

14. _____ cold   _____ hot   _____ carry   _____ hit

15. _____ flash   _____ fan   _____ fun   _____ garden

16. _____ seat   _____ sun   _____ saw   _____ sit

Add or subtract to solve each problem.

1. $9 - 3 =$ _____

2. $6 + 4 =$ _____

3. $5 + 3 =$ _____

4. $2 + 7 =$ _____

5. $8 - 2 =$ _____

6. $7 - 5 =$ _____

7. $4 + 5 =$ _____

8. $6 - 3 =$ _____

9. $6 + 3 =$ _____

10. $8 - 3 =$ _____

11. $9 - 4 =$ _____

12. $9 - 5 =$ _____

13. $5 + 4 =$ _____

14. $4 - 3 =$ _____

15. $7 + 2 =$ _____

CHARACTER CHECK: What is your best skill? What can you do to get even better at it?

ABC Book of Summer Adventures, Step 2

Keep track of the fun things you do this month. Each time you do one of your favorite things, take a picture or draw something to represent your adventure. Then, on this sheet, write a brief description of what you did. Continue on a separate sheet of paper. Also, if you would like, check items off your list of favorites on page 147 as you go.

1. _____

2. _____

3. _____

4. _____

5. _____

6. _____

7. _____

8. _____

9. _____

10. _____

Say the name of each picture. Draw a line to the letter that makes the same vowel sound.

a e i o u

Write each noun next to the correct box.

girl   truck   zoo
school   ball   baby

 **Person**

 **Place**

 **Thing**

Look at each clock. Write the time shown.

1.

2.

3.

_____ : _____   _____ : _____   _____ : _____

Write a number sentence to solve each problem.

4.

Four mittens sit on the shelf. Two mittens are taken. How many mittens are left?

_____ – _____ = _____

5.

Five hens sat in the coop. Two hens walked away. How many hens are left?

_____ – _____ = _____

FACTOID: In Sydney, Australia, it is 16 hours later than in New York City.

© Carson-Dellosa

Write the name of the animal that answers each riddle.

bear   camel   zebra   elephant   lion

1. I am big and brown. I sleep all winter. What am I?

    _____

2. I look like a horse with black and white stripes. What am I?

    _____

3. I have one or two humps on my back. Sometimes people ride on me.
    What am I?

    _____

4. I am a very big animal. I have a long nose called a trunk. What am I?

    _____

5. I have sharp claws and teeth. I am a great big cat. What am I?

    _____

Make the Effort!

With effort, you can get stronger, faster, and even smarter. Choose
something you would like to be better at and make a goal for yourself.
Maybe you want to run 100 yards in 30 seconds, learn a new song on
the piano, or know by heart all your addition facts through 10. Practice a
little every day until you achieve your goal.

Write a, e, i, o, or u on each line.

p_____g   c_____t   b_____t

h_____n   fr_____g   d_____ck

When you count pennies, you count by 1s. Count each set of pennies. Write the amount on each jar.

1.

2.

Add or subtract to solve each problem.

1.   7
    − 3

2.   3
    + 5

3.   9
    − 1

4.   6
    + 2

5.   5
    − 4

6.   7
    + 3

7.   6
    − 3

8.   8
    + 1

9.   5
    − 2

10.   4
    + 5

11.   9
    − 4

12.   4
    + 6

FITNESS FLASH: Sit down with the soles of your feet touching so that your legs look almost like butterfly wings. Hold your feet while you gently press your knees toward the floor. Hold for 20 seconds and then "flutter your wings" to release.

Rhyme Time

Read the nursery rhyme and clap to the beat. Then, write your own rhymes for verses 2, 3, and 4. Use a separate piece of paper, if needed.

Hickory, Dickory, Dock

Hickory, dickory, dock,
The mouse ran up the clock.
The clock struck one.
The mouse ran down!
Hickory, dickory, dock.

2. Hickory, dickory, dock,
    The mouse ran up the clock.
    The clock struck two.

    _____

    Hickory, dickory, dock.

3. Hickory, dickory, dock,
    The mouse ran up the clock.
    The clock struck three.

    _____

    Hickory, dickory, dock.

4. Hickory, dickory, dock,
    The mouse ran up the clock.
    The clock struck four.

    _____

    Hickory, dickory, dock.

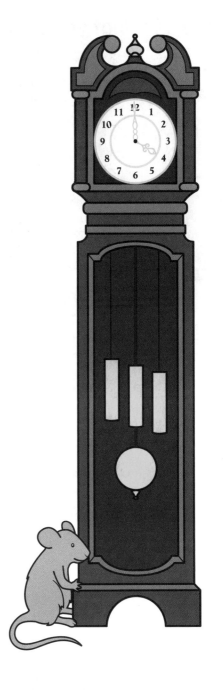

BONUS

Bubbles

You can have your own endless supply of bubbles, and just think—you can make them anytime you want!

What you'll need:

- $\frac{1}{2}$ cup glycerine (may be purchased at a pharmacy)
- $\frac{1}{2}$ cup water
- 1 tablespoon liquid dishwashing detergent
- Glass jar with a lid
- Bubble pipe, bubble wand, plastic drinking straws, twist ties, slotted spoons, or clothes hangers
- Baking pan (optional)

What to do:

1. Mix all the ingredients in a jar.

2. Make bubble wands out of twist ties, slotted spoons, clothes hangers, or straws.

3. Pour some of the bubble mix into a baking pan if you are making larger bubbles.

4. You can reuse the bubbles as long as you keep the jar tightly closed when you are finished playing.

5. Share your bubbles with a friend!

Circle the pairs that rhyme.

1.

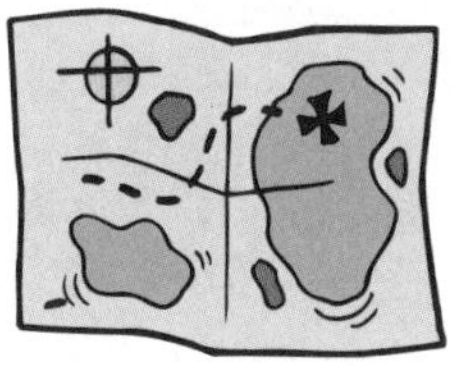

map   nest

2.

dog   frog

3.

hat   bat

4.

kite   mop

5.

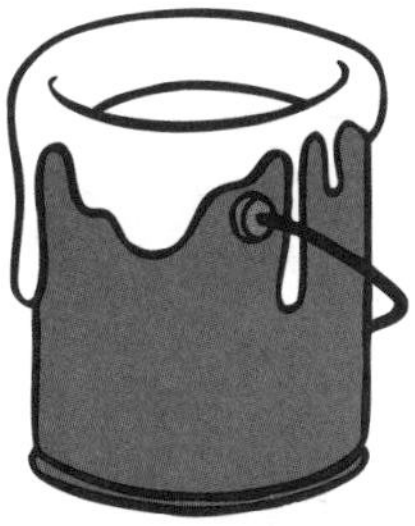

can   fan

6.

rat   pig

Write a number sentence to solve each story problem. Do not forget to write the + or – sign in the circle.

1. Together, Stephanie and Patricia planted **10** rows of green beans.
   Patricia planted **3** rows.
   How many rows did Stephanie plant?

_____ ◯ _____   = _____

2. Kyle and Marty picked **9** apples altogether.
   Marty picked **5** apples.
   How many apples did Kyle pick?

_____ ◯ _____   = _____

3. There were **6** ladybugs on a leaf.
   Later, **2** more ladybugs flew to the leaf.
   How many ladybugs were there in all?

_____ ◯ _____   = _____

FACTOID: A ladybug's spots fade as it ages.

Say each word. Listen for the long a sound. Draw Xs on the two words that do not have the long a sound.

bake	cane	cage	tap
cake	lane	page	cape
can	gate	rain	mane

A noun names a person, place, or thing. Circle two nouns in each sentence below. The first one is done for you.

The (pig) has a curly (tail.)

The hen is sitting on her nest.

A horse is in the barn.

The goat has horns.

Look at all four pictures in each row and circle the three that most belong together.

Add or subtract to solve each problem.

1. $9 - 3 =$ _____

2. $6 + 4 =$ _____

3. $5 + 3 =$ _____

4. $2 + 7 =$ _____

5. $8 - 2 =$ _____

6. $7 - 5 =$ _____

7. $4 + 5 =$ _____

8. $6 - 3 =$ _____

9. $6 + 3 =$ _____

10. $8 - 3 =$ _____

11. $9 - 4 =$ _____

12. $9 - 5 =$ _____

13. $5 + 4 =$ _____

14. $4 - 3 =$ _____

15. $7 + 2 =$ _____

When you count nickels, you count by 5s. Count each set of nickels. Write the total amount.

16.
  _____¢

17.   _____¢

18.   _____¢   _____¢

19. _____¢

Say the name of each picture. Write the letters you hear to spell each word.

1.

_____ _____ _____ e

2.

_____ _____ _____ e

3.

_____ _____ _____ e

4.

_____ _____ i _____

5.

_____ _____ i _____

6.

_____ _____ i _____ _____

REMINDER: Have you made any last adventures happen this month? Take another look at the list you started on page 148. See if you can do at least one more fun thing on your list before the summer is over.

Write the missing numbers in each fact family.

1. Family: 4, 5, 9

    $5 + \boxed{} = 9$

    $4 + 5 = \boxed{}$

    $9 - \boxed{} = 4$

    $9 - 4 = \boxed{}$

2. Family: 2, 8, 10

    $8 + \boxed{} = 10$

    $2 + 8 = \boxed{}$

    $10 - 2 = \boxed{}$

    $10 - \boxed{} = 8$

Look at each clock. Write the time shown.

3.

_____ : _____

4.

_____ : _____

5.

_____ : _____

FACTOID: In very hot and dry places, rain can evaporate before it hits the ground!

Draw a line from the sign to the sentence that tells about it.

1. If you see this sign, watch out for trains.

2. When cars or bikes come to this sign, they must stop.

3. When this sign is on, do not cross the street.

4. This sign tells you to stay out of the yard.

5. If you see this sign, do not eat or drink what is inside!

6. This sign warns you that it is not safe. Stay away!

7. This sign says you are not allowed to come in.

Say each word. Listen for the long e sound. Draw Xs on the two words that do not have the long e sound.

eel	queen	feet	rose
feel	seed	sweet	beak
pea	bead	red	beach

Dad and Ana are cooking. Circle the action word in each sentence that tells what they do.

1. Dad chops.

2. Ana mixes.

3. Ana stirs.

4. Ana washes.

5. Dad peels.

6. They bake.

CHARACTER CHECK: Think about how you can help your classmates next year. What can you teach others?

Circle one picture that most belongs with the first picture in each row.

Subtraction Color Code

Subtract to solve each problem. Then, use the code to color the spaces.

Color Code:

0 = green   **1** = brown   **2** = blue   **3** = purple   **4** = black   **5** = pink

BONUS

Tell Me More!

Find out what your friend loves more than anything in the world. Learn about what your family did before you were born. Discover your neighbor's greatest achievement. Practice your questioning skills and find out more!

Step 1: Think of someone you want to know more about. This should be a friend, family member, or neighbor you know and trust.

Step 2: Think of something you would like to know about that person. What are you curious about?

Step 3: Using the question words below, write at least one of each type of question. Work hard to make your questions about what you really want to find out.

Step 4: Set up your interview and ask away! Remember what you find out and share it with a friend or family member. You may also want to draw a picture of the person you interviewed.

Who _____ ?

What _____ ?

Where _____ ?

When _____ ?

Why _____ ?

Say the name of each picture. Write the letter of the beginning sound.

Example:

_____m_____

1.

_____

2.

_____

3.

_____

4.

_____

5.

_____

6.

_____

7.

_____

ABC

REMINDER: Which letters of the alphabet do you have an adventure for so far? Make sure you write a brief description of each adventure on the worksheet you started on page 153.

Say the name of each picture. Write the letters you hear to spell each word.

1.

_____ _____ _____ e

2.

_____ _____ _____ _____ e

3.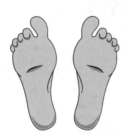

_____ _____ e _____

4.

_____ _____ a _____ _____

5.

_____ _____ a _____

6.

_____ _____ a _____

FACTOID: Toenails grow faster when it's hot outside.

Holding the first number in your head, count on your fingers to add each sum.

Example:
$$\begin{array}{r} 8 \\ + 5 \\ \hline \end{array}$$
Hold 8 in your head, and count 5 fingers while saying, "9, 10, 11, 12, 13." The sum is 13.

1.
$$\begin{array}{r} 7 \\ + 4 \\ \hline \end{array}$$

2.
$$\begin{array}{r} 10 \\ + 6 \\ \hline \end{array}$$

3.
$$\begin{array}{r} 13 \\ + 2 \\ \hline \end{array}$$

4.
$$\begin{array}{r} 12 \\ + 5 \\ \hline \end{array}$$

5.
$$\begin{array}{r} 8 \\ + 3 \\ \hline \end{array}$$

6.
$$\begin{array}{r} 9 \\ + 7 \\ \hline \end{array}$$

7.
$$\begin{array}{r} 6 \\ + 9 \\ \hline \end{array}$$

8.
$$\begin{array}{r} 2 \\ + 9 \\ \hline \end{array}$$

9.
$$\begin{array}{r} 4 \\ + 8 \\ \hline \end{array}$$

10.
$$\begin{array}{r} 5 \\ + 9 \\ \hline \end{array}$$

Add the pennies to the nickel in the jar. Write the total amount.

11.  $+$ 1¢ 1¢ 1¢ 1¢ 1¢ $=$ _____ ¢

12.  $+$ 1¢ 1¢ 1¢ 1¢ 1¢ 1¢ 1¢ 1¢ $=$ _____ ¢

Look at the picture. Circle the letter of the ending sound.

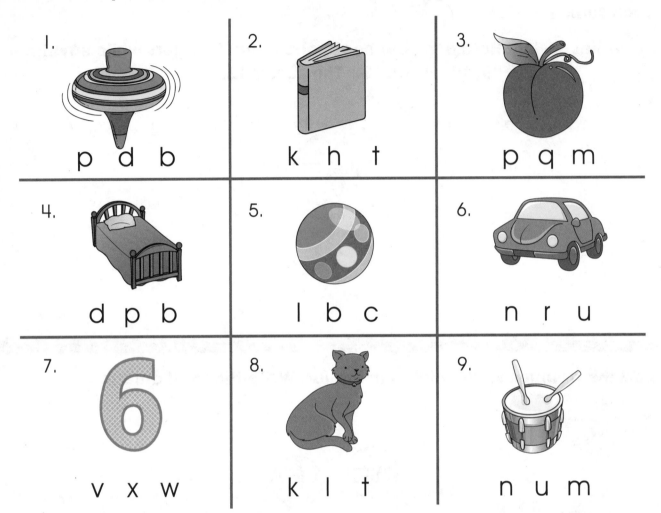

1. p d b

2. k h t

3. p q m

4. d p b

5. l b c

6. n r u

7. v x w

8. k l t

9. n u m

Happy and Healthy!

You may feel tired after school, but instead of sitting down to play video games or watch television, go outside and play for at least half an hour. If you're on your own, try playing hopscotch, jumping rope, kicking a soccer ball, or even making your own obstacle course. With friends, you might play tag, hide and seek, four square, or a game of football. Of course, you can always make up your own games, too! Being active and having fun are important for staying healthy and happy.

Say each word. Listen for the long i sound. Draw Xs on the two words that do not have the long i sound.

pie	wide	ripe	like
tip	side	pipe	hike
life	win	rise	mile

A verb is often an action word. Circle the verb in each sentence below.

1.

Two tiny dogs dance.

2.

The bear climbs a ladder.

3.

The clown falls down.

4.

A tiger jumps through a ring.

Holding the first number in your head, count backward on your fingers to find each difference.

Example:
$$\begin{array}{r} 11 \\ -\ 3 \\ \hline \end{array}$$

Hold 11 in your head, and count 3 fingers while saying, "10, 9, 8." The difference is 8.

1. $\begin{array}{r} 12 \\ -\ 2 \\ \hline \end{array}$
2. $\begin{array}{r} 15 \\ -\ 3 \\ \hline \end{array}$
3. $\begin{array}{r} 16 \\ -\ 1 \\ \hline \end{array}$
4. $\begin{array}{r} 11 \\ -\ 4 \\ \hline \end{array}$
5. $\begin{array}{r} 18 \\ -\ 3 \\ \hline \end{array}$

6. $\begin{array}{r} 20 \\ -\ 2 \\ \hline \end{array}$
7. $\begin{array}{r} 19 \\ -\ 5 \\ \hline \end{array}$
8. $\begin{array}{r} 17 \\ -\ 7 \\ \hline \end{array}$
9. $\begin{array}{r} 16 \\ -\ 9 \\ \hline \end{array}$
10. $\begin{array}{r} 20 \\ -\ 7 \\ \hline \end{array}$

Draw a minute hand and an hour hand on each clock to show the correct time.

time that I wake up

time that I go to bed

FITNESS FLASH: Do 10 jumping jacks.

178

Read the story. Then, answer the questions.

Ice-Cream Man

Hiro and Rose go to the park. The friendly ice-cream man is there selling ice-cream cones. "Hi, kids, would you two like an ice-cream cone?" he asks.

Rose and Hiro reach into their pockets, which are empty. "We don't have any money," says Rose.

The ice-cream man smiles at them and reaches into the freezer. "Well, look at that!" he says. "I have two extra cones right here! Someone has to eat them, and it may as well be you."

"Wow! Thanks!" say the kids, and they skip off with their treats.

1. What problem did Hiro and Rose have?

    a. They were very hot.

    b. They were lost in the park.

    c. They did not have any money.

2. How was the problem solved?

    a. The ice-cream man gave the kids free ice cream.

    b. The ice-cream man helped the kids find their way.

    c. The kids asked strangers for money.

3. Which word describes the ice-cream man?

    a. kind

    b. rude

    c. sad

Say the name of each picture. Write the letters you hear to spell each word.

1.

___ ___ ___ e

2.

___ ___ e

3.

___ ___ ___ e

4.

___ ___ ___ e

5.

___ ___ ___ e

6.

___ ___ ___ e

FACTOID: During the American Civil War, kites were used to deliver letters.

Add or subtract to solve each problem.

1. 7 + 3	2. 8 – 2	3. 9 – 5	4. 6 + 2	5. 5 + 3	6. 1 + 8
7. 6 – 3	8. 8 – 7	9. 9 + 1	10. 7 – 5	11. 9 – 4	12. 8 – 6
13. 3 + 6	14. 5 + 2	15. 9 – 2	16. 10 – 5	17. 10 – 8	18. 4 + 3

When you count dimes, you count by 10s. Count each set of dimes. Write the total amount.

19.

_____ ¢

20.

_____ ¢

21.

_____ ¢

22.

_____ ¢

Say the name of each picture. Write the correct beginning and ending sounds.

1.

_____

o

2.

_____

a

3.

_____

a

4.

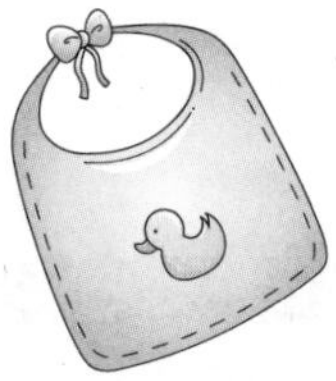

_____

i

5.

_____

u

6.

_____

e

CHARACTER CHECK: Think of three friends. What is one thing you like about each person?

Choose a New Ending!

Look at the picture story below.

Imagine a new ending to the story. Draw your ending in the box.

Grasping Objects

How do your thumbs help you grasp objects?

Materials

- tape
- pencil
- several small objects

Procedure

Have an adult help you tape the thumb of your writing hand to your palm so that you cannot move it. The tape should allow your other fingers to move freely. Try to pick up a pencil and write your name. Then, try to tie your shoes. Next, try to pick up each small object.

Remove the tape. Repeat each activity. Notice how your thumb works as you complete each activity.

1. Circle the activity that was easier.

    A. writing with a taped hand

    B. writing with no tape on your hand

2. Circle the activity that was more difficult.

    A. tying your shoe with no tape on your hand

    B. tying your shoe with a taped hand

3. Circle the names of the animals who have thumbs that help them grasp objects.

    monkey   fish

    frog   gorilla

Say each word. Listen for the long o sound. Draw Xs on the two words that do not have the long o sound.

hose	note	joke	bone
rose	page	poke	pod
toad	boat	roast	goat

A preposition can show where something is or which way it is going. Circle the preposition that matches each picture.

Dax passed the ball **from/to** Ella.

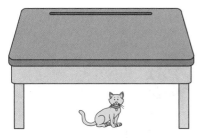

The cat is **under/next to** the desk.

The balloon is **after/above** the girl.

Holding the first number in your head, count on your fingers to add each sum.

Example: 6
+ 6

Hold 6 in your head, and count 6 fingers while saying, "7, 8, 9, 10, 11, 12." The sum is 12.

1.	8 + 4	2.	10 + 3	3.	9 + 2	4.	12 + 7	5.	8 + 8

6.	11 + 7	7.	9 + 9	8.	13 + 6	9.	4 + 9	10.	16 + 4

Circle the picture that rhymes with the first picture in each row.

11.

12.

13.

Say the name of each picture. Write the letters you hear to spell each word.

1.

_____ _____ a _____

2.

_____ _____ a _____

3.

_____ _____ a _____ _____

4.

_____ _____ a _____

5.

_____ _____ _____ e

6.

_____ _____ _____ e

FACTOID: Baby goats are called *kids*.

Holding the first number in your head, count backward on your fingers to find each difference.

Example: $\begin{array}{r} 14 \\ -\ 5 \end{array}$ **Hold 14 in your head, and count 5 fingers while saying, "13, 12, 11, 10, 9." The difference is 9.**

1. $\begin{array}{r} 16 \\ -\ 2 \end{array}$ 2. $\begin{array}{r} 13 \\ -\ 4 \end{array}$ 3. $\begin{array}{r} 16 \\ -\ 6 \end{array}$ 4. $\begin{array}{r} 11 \\ -\ 3 \end{array}$ 5. $\begin{array}{r} 17 \\ -\ 5 \end{array}$

6. $\begin{array}{r} 19 \\ -\ 6 \end{array}$ 7. $\begin{array}{r} 20 \\ -\ 5 \end{array}$ 8. $\begin{array}{r} 17 \\ -\ 4 \end{array}$ 9. $\begin{array}{r} 18 \\ -\ 9 \end{array}$ 10. $\begin{array}{r} 20 \\ -\ 10 \end{array}$

Fill in the blank with a word that rhymes with the underlined word.

11.

There is a <u>man</u> inside the _____.

12.

She likes to <u>run</u> under the _____.

FITNESS FLASH: Squat down to the floor and then pop up like popcorn. Do this 10 times.

188

ABC Book of Summer Adventures, Step 3

Make sure you have one summer activity for each letter of the alphabet. You may need to get creative with names for things. For example, for the letter X, maybe you list an "Extra Special Shopping Trip" or an "Exciting Day at the Beach." Write the name for each activity on the chart or on a separate sheet of paper if you need more room.

A		N	
B		O	
C		P	
D		Q	
E		R	
F		S	
G		T	
H		U	
I		V	
J		W	
K		X	
L		Y	
M		Z	

Summer Fun Puppet Show, Step 2

Return to your list of summer adventures on page 148. Cross off anything that did not happen this summer. Then, choose your three favorite adventures to turn into a puppet show. Who are the most important people in those adventures? They will become the puppets in your show. Make sure to include yourself and at least one other person.

Adventure 1: _____

What happened? _____

_____

_____

Most important people?

_____   _____

_____   _____

Adventure 2: _____

What happened? _____

_____

_____

Most important people?

_____   _____

_____   _____

Adventure 3: _____

What happened? _____

_____

_____

Most important people?

_____   _____

_____   _____

Lincoln counted the number of black, white, red, and green cars he saw on the way to the grocery store with his dad. He then drew a car for each one he saw. Color the graph to show how many cars of each color Lincoln saw.

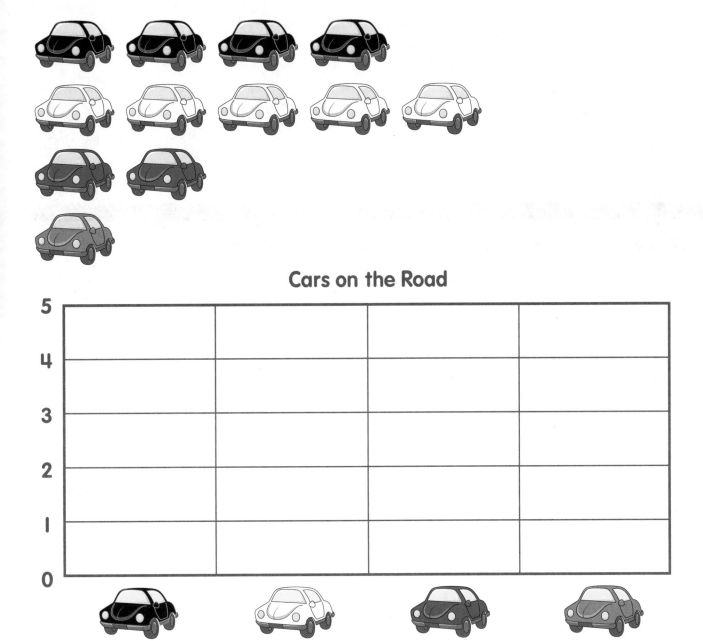

Cars on the Road

Lincoln saw fewer _____ cars than any other color.

Solve for the missing number in each equation. Write the number in the box.

1. 6
    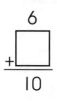
    10

2. 3

    8

3.
    + 4
    9

4. □
    + 5
    7

5. 8

    9

6. 7

    10

7. □
    + 2
    8

8. □
    + 5
    10

Write what makes you happy. Write what makes you sad.

_____

- -

_____ makes me happy.

_____

- -

_____ makes me sad.

Say each word. Listen for the long u sound. Draw Xs on the two words that do not have the long u sound.

cute	tune	fume	music
tub	mule	fuse	cube
up	mute	tube	juice

Choose a preposition to complete each sentence. Write it on the line.

off	into	in

_____

Ling hid _____ the shed.

at	on	up

_____

The cat can jump _____ the table.

Solve for the missing number in each equation. Write the number in the box.

1.
```
   9
 -☐
 ───
   3
```

2.
```
  10
 -☐
 ───
   7
```

3.
```
  ☐
 - 4
 ───
   4
```

4.
```
  ☐
 - 7
 ───
   2
```

5.
```
  10
 -☐
 ───
   1
```

6.
```
   7
 -☐
 ───
   3
```

7.
```
  ☐
 - 5
 ───
   2
```

8.
```
  ☐
 - 10
 ───
   0
```

Use the letters in the box to see how many words you can make. You will use each letter more than once.

| b | m | n | p | r | s | t |

p an   _____ at   _____ in

_____ an   _____ at   _____ in

_____ an   _____ at   _____ ug

_____ an   _____ at   _____ ug

_____ ut   _____ et   _____ op

_____ ut   _____ et   _____ op

Table Fort

Read the story. Then, answer the questions.

"Mom, can we build a fort in the dining room?" John asked.

"Sure, Honey," said John's mom. Then, the two found a giant sheet and covered the dining room table with it.

The fort was built! The only problem was the door to the fort would not stay shut. John tried putting pillows on top, but the sheet kept slipping open.

John's mom said, "We need something stronger to hold these ends together."

"I'll be right back!" said John, and he ran to the laundry room. He came back with three clothespins. John and his mom used them to clip the ends of the sheet together.

"Yes! It worked!" said John. "Let's eat lunch inside the fort!"

1. What problem did John and his mom have?
   a. John wanted to build a fort, but his mom did not.
   b. The dining room table was covered in pillows.
   c. The door to the fort would not stay closed.

2. How was the problem solved?
   a. John found clothespins to clip the sheet's ends together.
   b. John begged his mom to let him build a fort.
   c. John helped his mom put the pillows away.

3. Which sentence best describes John and his mom?
   a. They work well together.
   b. They do not agree.
   c. They do not like messes.

FITNESS FLASH: Do a silly dance for 60 seconds. See how fast you can move your arms and legs!

Say the name of each picture. Write the letter sounds you hear to spell each word.

1.

   ____ ____ s ____ c

2.

   ____ ____ ____ e

3.

   ___ ____ ____ e

4.

   ____ ____ ____ e

5.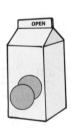

   ___ ____ i c e

6.

   ____ n i ____ o r ____

FACTOID: Because there is no air there, it is impossible to make music on the moon.

Moon Code

Max is pretending to fly through the solar system. He wants to visit more moons.

Use the code to discover the names of some moons in our solar system.

A	B	C	D	E	F	G	H	I	J	K	L	M
1	2	3	4	5	6	7	8	9	10	11	12	13

N	O	P	Q	R	S	T	U	V	W	X	Y	Z
14	15	16	17	18	19	20	21	22	23	24	25	26

First, he sees Jupiter's moon named ___ ___. It has at least eight active
volcanoes.   9   15

___ ___ ___ ___ ___ ___ travels around Mars in 7 $\frac{1}{2}$ hours. No other moon
 16   8   15   2   15   19

travels so fast!

Next, he goes to the largest moon in the solar system.

It is named ___ ___ ___ ___ ___ ___ ___ ___. It orbits Jupiter.
             7   1   14 25 13   5   4   5

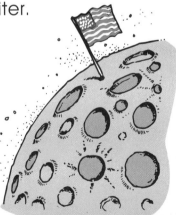

Changing Matter

Matter can change forms. Sometimes, a liquid becomes a solid, and a solid becomes a liquid. Try the simple experiment below.

Materials

- Water
- Ice tray
- Freezer

Procedure

1. Pour water into an ice tray. Touch the liquid.

2. Put the water in a freezer for two hours.

3. Take it out. Touch it. What does it feel like now?

_____

- -

The liquid became a _____ .

Now...

1. Take the ice cubes outside on a warm, sunny day.

2. Leave them in the sun for two hours.

3. Now, touch the ice cubes.

_____

- -

The solid became a _____ .

Ada went to the farmers' market with her family. They picked out 5 ears of corn, 2 pumpkins, 3 eggplants, and I head of lettuce. Color the graph to show how many of each vegetable Ada's family bought.

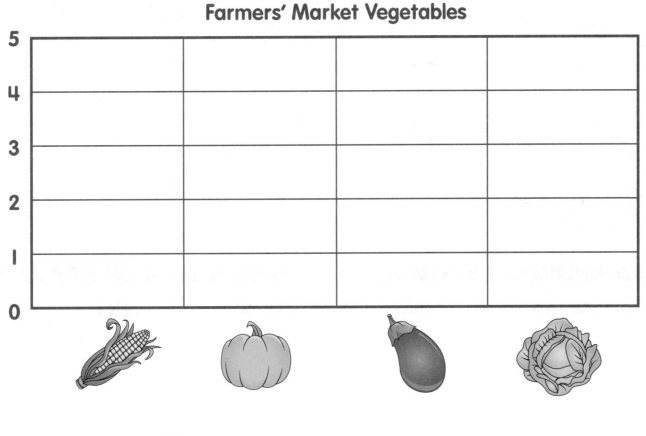

Farmers' Market Vegetables

Ada's family bought more _____ than any other vegetable.

Get Ready For School!

Next school year, become more independent! Be on time and ready for school each day all by yourself. To reach this goal, try making a schedule of your morning. Think about what tasks you have to complete before leaving for school, including any items you need to pack. Then, draw a picture of each task, label it, and write what time it will happen each morning. Begin your schedule with waking up and end it with leaving for school.

Number the objects as follows: I – long, 2 – medium, 3 – short.

1.

_____

_____

_____

2.

_____

_____

_____

3.

_____

_____

_____

4.

_____

_____

_____

Write the two words that make up each compound word below.

5.

airplane

_____ _____

- -

_____ _____

6.

watermelon

_____ _____

- -

_____ _____

7.

haircut

_____ _____

- -

_____ _____

200

Add or subtract to solve each problem.

1. 5 + 2 = _____

2. 9 – 3 = _____

3. 9 + 1 = _____

4. 7 – 4 = _____

5. 6 + 2 = _____

6. 8 – 5 = _____

7. 4 + 5 = _____

8. 10 – 2 = _____

9. 7 + 3 = _____

10. 8 – 4 = _____

11. 5 + 5 = _____

12. 6 – 3 = _____

13. 10 + 0 = _____

14. 6 – 4 = _____

15. 5 + 3 = _____

Say the name of each picture. Circle the number that tells how many syllables are in each name.

16.

1   2

17.

1   2

18.

1   2

CHARACTER CHECK: Make an effort to say hello to your classmates on the first day of school, even the ones you don't know.

Use the paper clips to measure each object.

1.

_____ paper clips

2.

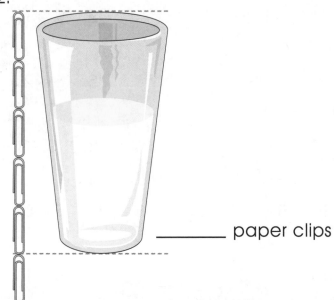

_____ paper clips

Underline the two words in each sentence that can make a compound word. Write the compound word on the line to complete the sentence.

3.

A kind of bird that is black is a

_____

_____ .

4.

A horse that can race is a

_____

_____ .

5.

A cloth that covers a table is a

_____

_____ .

Add or subtract to solve each probem.

1. 2
  + 3
	2. 4
	  + 4
		3. 5
		  + 2
			4. 6
			  + 3
				5. 3
				  + 4

6. 4
  − 1
	7. 8
	  − 6
		8. 9
		  − 5
			9. 6
			  − 2
				10. 7
				  − 6

Write the missing numbers.

1	2		4					
					16		19	
	22	23						
							39	
		44						50
	52							

Summer Fun Puppet Show, Step 3

Make puppets for each character in your puppet show. Use the directions below for paper bag puppets or make puppets out of socks, craft sticks, or cardboard tubes.

Materials

- paper lunch bag
- newpapers
- yarn or craft fur
- dowel rod, wooden spoon, or a ruler
- crayons or markers
- construction paper
- glue
- plastic wiggly eyes (optional)

Summer Fun Puppet Show, Step 3 (continued)

Directions

1. Hold the dowel rod in the center of the bag. Fill the bag with crumpled newspaper around the rod, as shown.

2. Tie the bag's opening tightly with yarn. Turn the bag upside down so that the yarn is at the bottom.

3. Using construction paper and crayons, create a face on your puppet.

4. Use yarn to make hair.

Suggestion

Put your hand inside the bag and make your puppet talk. Decorate it with eyes, hair, a tongue, and so on.

205

Color the kittens using the clues below.

The first kitten wears silver bracelets and purple boots. It is pushing on the ball of green yarn.

The second kitten is lounging on top of the ball of green yarn. It is wearing a blue T-shirt.

The third kitten wears a red top hat. It is pulling on the ball of green yarn.

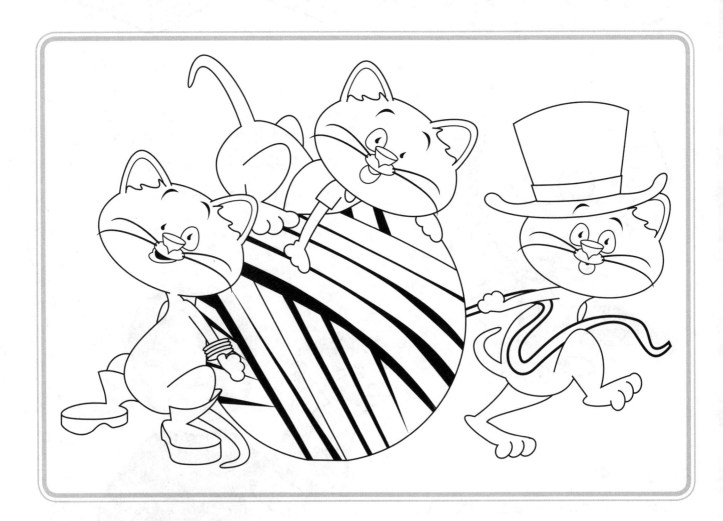

FITNESS FLASH: Lie on your back with your legs straight. Lift both legs at the same time and slowly lower them until they are almost touching the floor. Hold for 10 seconds.

Add or subtract to solve each problem. Use the ten frames for help.

1. $\begin{array}{r} 14 \\ + \ 5 \end{array}$ $\begin{array}{r} + \end{array}$

2. $\begin{array}{r} 15 \\ - \ 5 \end{array}$ $\begin{array}{r} - \end{array}$

3. $\begin{array}{r} 17 \\ + \ 3 \end{array}$ $\begin{array}{r} + \end{array}$

4. $\begin{array}{r} 14 \\ - \ 2 \end{array}$ $\begin{array}{r} - \end{array}$

5. $\begin{array}{r} 12 \\ + \ 2 \end{array}$ $\begin{array}{r} + \end{array}$

6. $\begin{array}{r} 20 \\ - \ 4 \end{array}$ $\begin{array}{r} - \end{array}$

7. $\begin{array}{r} 10 \\ + \ 7 \end{array}$ $\begin{array}{r} + \end{array}$

8. $\begin{array}{r} 20 \\ - \ 1 \end{array}$ $\begin{array}{r} - \end{array}$

9. $\begin{array}{r} 11 \\ + \ 4 \end{array}$ $\begin{array}{r} + \end{array}$

10. $\begin{array}{r} 17 \\ - \ 7 \end{array}$ $\begin{array}{r} - \end{array}$

Draw lines between pictures that rhyme.

 **3**

Write the missing numbers.

61	62								
				75					
		83							
									100
101									110
				115					120

© Carson-Dellosa

Read the passage. Then, answer the questions.

Penguins

Penguins are birds, but they cannot fly. Instead, penguins are very good swimmers and spend a lot of time in the water. Their wings help them swim! Penguins' wings are really more like flippers, which they flap to swim. Most penguins can swim up to 7 miles per hour. Some penguins can swim as fast as 22 miles per hour! Other animals in the water hunt penguins, so penguins need to be extra fast. Penguins' white belly feathers and black back feathers make it hard for other animals to spot them. This helps keep penguins safe.

1. Which sentence tells the main idea?
   a. Penguins are birds that swim but don't fly.
   b. Penguins are hunted by other animals.
   c. Penguins' wings work like flippers.

2. Which detail from the passage tells one reason penguins swim fast?
   a. Penguins are birds, but they cannot fly.
   b. Most penguins can swim up to 7 miles per hour.
   c. Other animals in the water hunt penguins.

3. According to the passage, which detail about penguins is true?
   a. Some penguins can fly.
   b. Penguins are great swimmers.
   c. Penguins spend most of their time on land.

4. Write a title for the passage that shows the main idea.

_____

FACTOID: Rockhopper penguins bounce up into their nests.

Write your name. Make each letter into a picture.

ABC Book of Summer Adventures, Final Step

You are ready to make your ABC book! Follow the directions below.

Materials

- your pictures and drawings of summer adventures
- 15 sheets of paper (You will use both sides of each sheet, so you will need 13 for your alphabetized pages plus 2 for your cover.) Choose paper that is large enough to hold your pictures and still leave room for words.
- glue or tape
- markers, colored pencils, or crayons
- stapler

Directions

1. Put your pictures in order according to your list on page 189. If a picture needs to be drawn and colored again, do that. Then, make any final tweaks.
2. Decide what to write at the top of each page. Each page should include the letter of the alphabet and a name for what is pictured (example: *T: Three-legged Race*).
3. Write the words that go on each page, making sure to leave enough room for the picture.
4. Glue or tape your pictures to their matching pages.
5. Make a front and back cover for your book. Be sure to include the title and author (That's you!) on the front cover.
6. Ask an adult to staple your book together.

ABC Book of Summer Adventures
Finished Product Examples

Have fun with the design of your ABC Book! Here are two different ways to lay out your pages:

These pages have the letter of the alphabet at the top and the name of the activity on the bottom. Also, notice that two of the pages (for Q and X) use descriptive words to fit the letter of the alphabet.

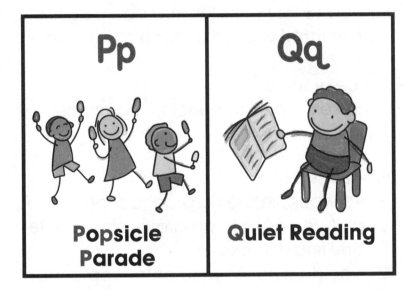

These pages hide the letter of the alphabet within each picture. To follow this example, you may find shapes that look like letters in your drawings and make those shapes stand out. If you don't see any letter shapes in your drawings, you could add something to each drawing that has the shape of the letter you need.

Summer Fun Puppet Show, Final Step

You are ready to write your puppet show! Follow the directions below.

Materials

- your three favorite adventures from page 190
- puppets for each character
- paper and pencil
- friends or family members to help

Directions

1. Answer out loud the questions below about your three favorite summer adventures. You don't need to write your answers unless you would like to.
2. Choose the most important event from each adventure to turn into a play.
3. Think about how to show the action step-by-step with your puppets.
4. Then, think about what your puppets can say to each other to help tell the story.
5. Write down the words and actions for each puppet. Look at the example on the next page for how to do that.

Prewriting Questions

What are the three summer adventures you chose for your puppet show?

What happened on each adventure?

Did anyone have a problem? If so, was it solved? How?

What was the most exciting part of each adventure?

What details does the audience need to know to understand the most exciting part of each adventure? Think about how you can show and tell just enough for your story to make sense.

Summer Fun Puppet Show
Finished Product Example

Here is an example of one puppet play. (Remember that you need three plays to make up your show.) The author does not tell about her whole day at the beach. Instead, she chooses the most exciting part—when she and her dad made a sand princess. Notice how the author includes both what the puppets say and the actions that they do.

Sand Princess

Dad: Do you want to build a sand castle?

Sara: No, let's build a sand princess!

Dad: How do we do that?

Sara: I'll show you. Start with her face.

[Dad and Sara make shaping and patting motions in the "sand."]

Dad: Ahhh.

Sara: Then, make her dress and shoes.

Dad: Like this?

[Dad and Sara make more shaping and patting motions.]

Sara: Yep! Now, we have to add her crown!

[Sara shapes and pats the crown.]

Sara: Mom! Come see what we made!

[Mom comes over.]

Mom: Wow! She's beautiful! Oh, no! Here comes a wave!

[Puppets run off the stage.]

B is for Butterfly!

Practice following directions. Ask an adult to read these directions to you as you do the actions. You will need a sheet of paper, a pencil, and crayons.

Step 1: Starting two inches (or about the width of four thumbs) from the top of the page, write a big uppercase B in the center of your paper.

Step 2: Turn your paper so that the humps of the B are sitting on top of the straight line of the B.

Step 3: Make the straight line longer by the width of one pointer finger on each end.

Step 4: Turn the straight line into a long, thin oval, like a skinny hot dog.

Step 5: Draw a small circle (a little wider than the oval) on the left end of the oval.

Step 6: Draw a small letter V on top of the circle, so that the point of the V rests on the circle.

Did you make a butterfly?

Step 7: Use crayons to finish the butterfly and decorate the wings.

BONUS

First-Grade Goals

Make sure you have the best possible year in first grade! Set goals for the new school year and work toward achieving them.

What skills would you like to make progress in by the end of the year? Are you shy about asking questions? If so, set a goal to ask at least one question per day. Do you love to read? Set a reading goal. How many books can you read each week? Maybe you have a hard time staying organized. A good goal might be to clear out your backpack every night before bed.

List your first-grade goals here. Then, check back during the school year to track your success! As you meet your goal each month, put a checkmark in one of the small boxes. At the end of the year, you can draw a star in the big box to show you met your goal for the school year.

Goal 1 _____

| 1 | 2 | 3 | 4 | 5 | 6 | 7 | 8 | 9 | |

Goal 2 _____

| 1 | 2 | 3 | 4 | 5 | 6 | 7 | 8 | 9 | |

Goal 3 _____

| 1 | 2 | 3 | 4 | 5 | 6 | 7 | 8 | 9 | |

Answer Key

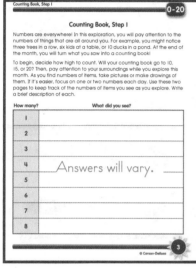

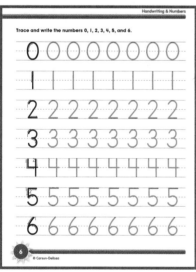

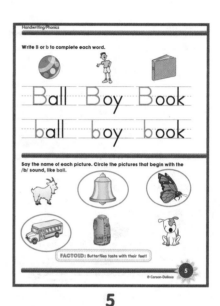

3

4

5

6

7

8

Answer Key

Write D or d to complete each word.

Door Dog Desk

door dog desk

Say the name of each picture. Circle the pictures that begin with the /d/ sound, like dog.

FACTOID: Not all ducks quack. Some grunt, squeal, or even whistle!

13

Trace and write the numbers 7, 8, 9, 10, 11, 12, and 13.

7 7 7 7 7 7 7 7 7

8 8 8 8 8 8 8 8

9 9 9 9 9 9 9 9

10 10 10 10 10 10

11 11 11 11 11 11

12 12 12 12 12 12

13 13 13 13 13

14

Write F or f to complete each word.

Fish Fan Fox

fish fan fox

Say the name of each picture. Circle the pictures that begin with the /f/ sound, like fish.

15

square rectangle triangle rhombus circle oval

Color the shapes to match the shapes at the top of the page.

16

Write G or g to complete each word.

Gum Goat Gate

gum goat gate

Say the name of each picture. Circle the pictures that begin with the /g/ sound, like gum.

FACTOID: Guitar strings are so strong that they can be used to cut chocolate.

17

Shapes in the Wild, Step 2

When you are out and about, look for squares, rectangles, triangles, rhombuses, circles, and ovals. If you can, carry your decorated shapes with you in a folder or notebook. When you see a shape in real life, take a picture of it or draw it, and include the matching decorated shape in each picture. Keep track of the shapes you find on the sheet below.

Shape	Where did you find the shape? Was it part of something else?
☐	
☐	
△	Answers will vary.
◇	
○	
○	

18

Answer Key

Write H or h to complete each word.

Hand Hat Ham

hand hat ham

Say the name of each picture. Circle the pictures that begin with the /h/ sound, like hand.

21

Count the number of objects in each set. Write the number on the line.

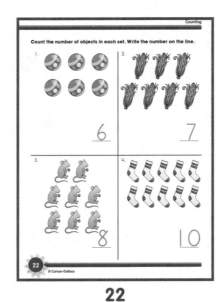

1.
2. 6
3. 7
4. 8   10

22

Write J or j to complete each word.

Jet Jar Jam

jet jar jam

Say the name of each picture. Circle the pictures that begin with the /j/ sound, like jet.

FITNESS FLASH: Squat and hop like a frog 10 times.

23

Complete each shape to match the first shape in each row.

1.
2.
3.
4.

24

Write K or k to complete each word.

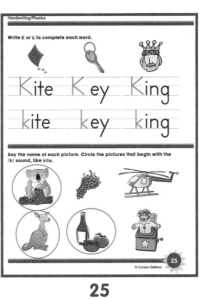

Kite Key King

kite key king

Say the name of each picture. Circle the pictures that begin with the /k/ sound, like kite.

25

Trace and write the numbers 14, 15, 16, 17, 18, 19, and 20.

14 14 14 14 14
15 15 15 15 15
16 16 16 16 16
17 17 17 17 17
18 18 18 18 18
19 19 19 19 19
20 20 20 20 20

26

Answer Key

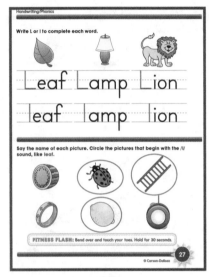

27

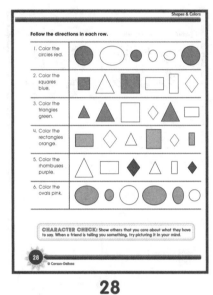

28

29

30

32

33

Answer Key

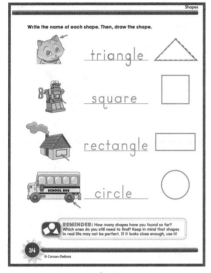

34

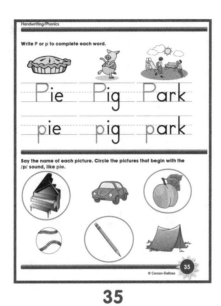

35

36

37

38

39

Answer Key

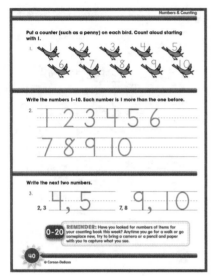

40

41

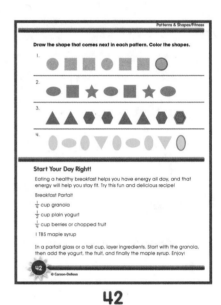

42

BONUS

Social Studies Activity

Communication Today

Look at the hand-written letter. In the past, if people wanted to keep in touch, they had to write and mail letters. Draw one faster way we use to communicate today.

PAST

PRESENT

Answers will vary.

44

Handwriting/Phonics

Write T or t to complete each word.

Top   Tent   Tiger

top   tent   tiger

Say the name of each picture. Circle the pictures that begin with the /t/ sound, like top.

45

Counting

Count the sets in each box. Color the set that has more.

46

Answer Key

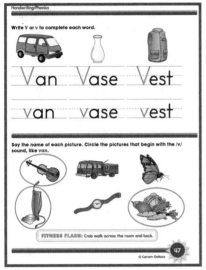

47

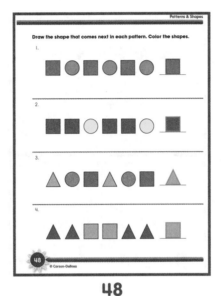

48

49

50

51

52

Answer Key

53

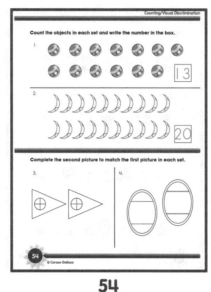

54

55

56

57

58

Answer Key

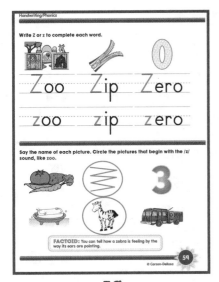

59

60

61

62

63

64

225

Answer Key

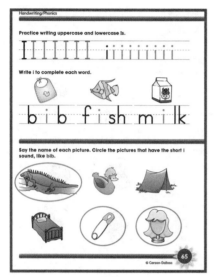

65

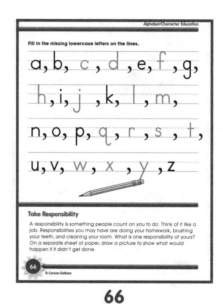

66

67

68

73

77

Answer Key

Animal Tracker, Step 1

Learn about animals just by observing them! In this exploration, you will look and listen for animals wherever you go. When you see a new animal, you will take or draw a picture of it and write a short description. Then, at the end of the month, you will use your findings to make a guidebook about animals!

Use this sheet to keep track of the animals you see and hear this month. Look for animals in your yard, in the neighborhood, in nearby parks, or wherever your travels take you. Take pictures or draw the animals you see. Then, write the animal's name, where it was found, what it was doing, and any sounds it made. Continue on a separate sheet of paper, if needed. If you don't know the name of the animal, your picture should help you find out.

Animal	Where Found	Animal's Actions and Sounds
	Answers will vary.	

78

78

Say the name of each picture. Write a to complete each word that has the short a sound heard in cat.

1. ant
2. fan
3. t p
4. map
5. cat
6. j t

79

79

Color the spaces on the umbrella. Use the number key to help you.

1 3 5 7 = yellow
2 4 6 8 = purple

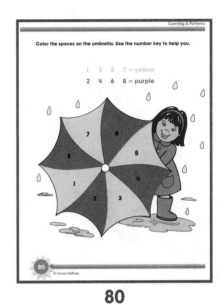

80

80

Imagine what it's like to be someone in the picture. Describe something you see, hear, smell, taste, and touch. Use words that show what you picture in your mind.

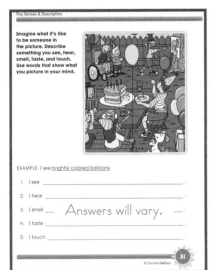

EXAMPLE: I see brightly colored balloons.

1. I see ___
2. I hear ___
3. I smell ___ Answers will vary. ___
4. I taste ___
5. I touch ___

81

81

Add to find each sum.

1. $3 + 1 = 4$
2. $4 + 1 = 5$
3. $3 + 0 = 3$
4. $2 + 2 = 4$
5. $1 + 3 = 4$
6. $5 + 0 = 5$
7. $1 + 4 = 5$
8. $2 + 3 = 5$
9. $1 + 1 = 2$

Say each word. Listen for the short a sound. Draw an X on the words that do not have the short a sound.

cap

ant   pig ✗
sad   bed ✗
make ✗   can
had   tag

FACTOID: The first baseball hats were made out of straw.

82

82

Look at the pictures below. Draw a line to match each picture to its opposite.

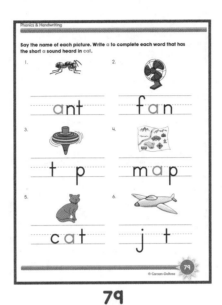

83

83

© Carson-Dellosa

Answer Key

Connect each set of shapes as shown to make a new shape. Circle the new shape.

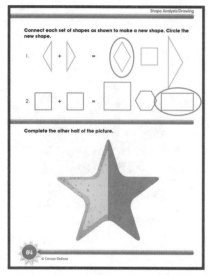

Complete the other half of the picture.

84

Write the next number in each set.

1. | 5 | 6 | 7 |
2. | 2 | 3 | 4 |
3. | 17 | 18 | 19 |

Read each sentence aloud. Listen for the short a sound. Circle each word that has the short a sound.

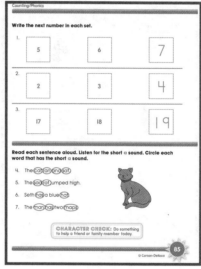

4. The cat ran and sat.
5. The sad rat jumped high.
6. Seth has a blue hat.
7. The man has two maps.

CHARACTER CHECK: Do something to help a friend or family member today.

85

Color each picture the correct color.

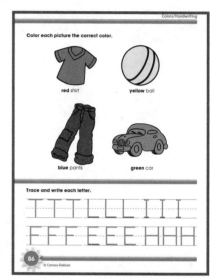

red shirt   **yellow** ball

blue pants   **green** car

Trace and write each letter.

T T T L L L I I I
F F F E E E H H H

86

Add to find each sum. Place beans on the jar below to help you solve the problems.

1. 6 + 1 = 7
2. 8 + 2 = 10
3. 5 + 4 = 9
4. 3 + 6 = 9
5. 9 + 1 = 10
6. 7 + 3 = 10
7. 5 + 3 = 8
8. 4 + 2 = 6

Take Charge of Your Learning!

Make a list of things you want to know more about. Write down what you already know about each topic. Then, write what else you would like to find out.

The next time you're at the library, check out a book or magazine that will help you learn what you want to know.

87

Read the poem. Underline all the words that have the short a sound. Then, answer the questions.

Imagine That!

What would you say
to a bat in a hat
if he asked you to play
in a stack made of hay?

What if the plan
was to skate with a cat
by the lake where the man
with the fan gets a tan?

Would you hop in a cab?
Catch a train with your dad?
Or be glad to be asked?
Grab a snack! Have a blast!

1. What event from the poem does the picture show?
   a. skating with a cat
   b. playing in a haystack
   c. catching a train

2. Which way to leave is not named in the poem?
   a. catching a train
   b. taking a cab
   c. riding a bus

FACTOID: The inventor of roller skates crashed into a mirror the first time he wore them in public.

88

BONUS

Declare Your Independence!

On the Fourth of July, we celebrate our country's independence. One way the U.S. shows its independence is by flying the nation's flag. The stars, stripes, and colors represent our 50 states, the 13 original colonies, and the things that are important to our country.

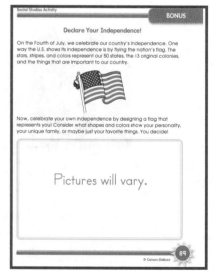

Now, celebrate your own independence by designing a flag that represents you! Consider what shapes and colors show your personality, your unique family, or maybe just your favorite things. You decide!

Pictures will vary.

89

Answer Key

91

Phonics & Handwriting

Say the name of each picture. Write *e* to complete each word that has the short *e* sound heard in *egg*.

1. b_ll
2. t e nt
3. h e n
4. v e st
5. t e n
6. b_b

92

Counting

On each number line, draw a dot on the first even number. Then, skip count by 2s. Draw a dot on each even number in the pattern. The first pattern has been started for you.

1. 0 1 2 3 4 5 6 7 8 9 10

2. 9 10 11 12 13 14 15 16 17 18 19

Now, skip count by 10s. Draw a dot on each multiple of 10. The pattern has been started for you.

3. 10 11 12 13 14 15 16 17 18 19 20 21 22 23 24 25 26 27 28 29 30 31 32 33 34 35 36 37 38 39 40

FITNESS FLASH: Hop on one leg 10 times. Then, switch legs.

93

Writing

Writing an Opinion

When you write about your opinion, your goal should be to persuade others to think what you think. In order to get your audience to agree with you, you have to provide reasons for the way you feel.

Practice providing reasons for your opinion. First, think of a game that you really like to play. Use the graphic organizer below to give four reasons for liking that game. Follow the example.

EXAMPLE

- players can use strategies
- fast-paced
- Ping Pong
- ball makes a cool sound
- players have to focus

Answers will vary.

94

Subtraction/Phonics

Subtract to find each difference.

1. 3 − 1 = 2
2. 3 − 2 = 1
3. 4 − 2 = 2
4. 4 − 1 = 3
5. 5 − 4 = 1
6. 5 − 3 = 2
7. 2 − 1 = 1
8. 4 − 3 = 1
9. 4 − 0 = 4

Say each word. Listen for the short *e* sound. Draw an X on the words that do not have the short *e* sound.

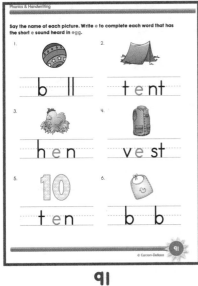

bed

pet   ten

~~meet~~   jet

~~bag~~   net

web   ~~team~~

FACTOID: Not all spiders spin webs.

95

Classification

Circle the three objects that most belong together in each row.

96

Shape Analysis/Drawing

Divide each rectangle into two triangles. Color one triangle blue and the other triangle yellow.

Complete the other half of the picture.

Answer Key

Write the first number in each set.

1. 7, 8, 9
2. 13, 14, 15
3. 18, 19, 20

Read each sentence aloud. Listen for the short e sound. Circle each word that has the short e sound.

4. (Jed) is in his (bed).
5. (Peg) has a (pet) (hen).
6. (Ben) and (Wes) have five toy (jets).
7. (Beth) has a (red) (pen).

FITNESS FLASH: Do 10 push-ups.

97

Color each picture the correct color.

orange block
pink pig
purple balloon
brown bear

Trace and write each letter.

a a a d d d g g g
c c c q q q e e e

98

Subtract to find each difference. Place beans on the jar below to help you solve the problems.

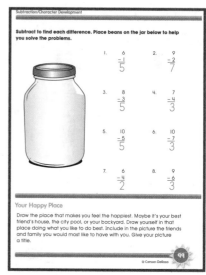

1. 6 − 1 = 5
2. 9 − 2 = 7
3. 8 − 3 = 5
4. 7 − 4 = 3
5. 10 − 5 = 5
6. 10 − 7 = 3
7. 6 − 4 = 2
8. 9 − 6 = 3

Your Happy Place

Draw the place that makes you feel the happiest. Maybe it's your best friend's house, the city pool, or your backyard. Draw yourself in that place doing what you like to do best. Include in the picture the friends and family you would most like to have with you. Give your picture a title.

99

Read the poem. Underline all the words that have the short e sound. Then, answer the questions.

Heading West

Ben dressed in red pants and a vest,
Packed his bags, and left for the West.
He knew it was time that he went
When a bird made a nest in his tent.

No, Ben did not feel so safe in his bed
With a bird hanging over his head.
So he jumped in his jeep with a yell.
And sped off to a new place to dwell*.

*dwell v. to live

1. What color are Ben's pants?
   a. blue
   b. black
   c. red

2. Why is Ben leaving?
   a. Ben does not like camping.
   b. A bird is in Ben's tent.
   c. Ben misses his family.

3. How is Ben getting to the West?
   a. in a jeep
   b. on an airplane
   c. on a bicycle

4. In the last line of the poem, what does "sped off" mean?
   a. jumped high
   b. went away fast
   c. dropped something

REMINDER: Have you looked for new animals this week? Anytime you go someplace where animals might be, try to bring a camera and pencil and paper with you. That way, you can record what the animal looks like and any sounds it makes.

100

BONUS

Symbols on Maps

A symbol is a picture that stands for something that is shown on a map. Symbols used in a map are shown in the Map Key. Look at the symbols. Draw a line from each symbol to what it stands for in the drawing below.

Map Key

101

Say the name of each picture. Write i to complete each word that has the short i sound heard in fish.

1. w i g
2. s i x
3. s n
4. w b
5. p i n
6. sh i p

103

© Carson-Dellosa

Answer Key

Make a pet chart. Ask 20 people if they have a pet.
Use tally marks to show what kind.

				Other	None

Tally Marks
I = 1
II = 2
III = 3
IIII = 4
IIII = 5

Use your pet chart. Write the number.

How many people have 🐕? _____

How many people have 🐈? _____

How man

How man   Answers will vary.

How many people do not have a pet? _____

How many people have a pet that is not on the chart? _____

Complete.

Which pet is the favorite? _____

Which pet is the least favorite? _____

CHARACTER CHECK: Sometimes, it is frustrating not to understand something. What can you do when you don't understand?

104

104

Imagine what it's like to be someone in the picture. Describe something you see, hear, smell, taste, and touch. Use words that show what you picture in your mind.

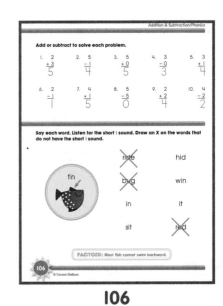

EXAMPLE: I hear <u>waves crashing on the sand</u>.

1. I see _____

2. I hear _____

3. I smell — Answers will vary. —

4. I taste _____

5. I touch _____

105

105

Add or subtract to solve each problem.

1.	2	2.	5	3.	5	4.	3	5.	3
	+3		−1		+0		−0		+1
	5		4		5		3		4

6.	2	7.	4	8.	5	9.	2	10.	4
	−1		+1		−5		+2		−2
	1		5		0		4		2

Say each word. Listen for the short i sound. Draw an X on the words that do not have the short i sound.

fin

~~ride~~   hid

~~big~~   win

in   it

sit   ~~red~~

FACTOID: Most fish cannot swim backward.

106

106

The sentence below uses all letters of the alphabet. Use it to practice your handwriting.

The wizard's very big ox jumped quickly for change.

The wizard's
very big ox
jumped quickly
for change.

107

107

Color the shapes to match the shapes above.

Circle the picture that shows the cat over the dog.

Circle the picture that shows the truck next to the toy box.

108

108

Add or subtract to solve each problem. Use the 10 dots below to help you solve.

1.	10	2.	9	3.	3	4.	5
	−6		−9		+5		+1
	4		0		8		6

5.	4	6.	10	7.	7	8.	10
	+2		−5		+3		−8
	6		5		10		2

9.	7	10.	6	11.	9	12.	2
	−4		+4		−7		+5
	3		10		2		7

Read each sentence aloud. Listen for the short i sound. Circle each word that has the short i sound.

13. Jim hid the bib in a bag.

14. The fish swim in the pond.

15. The big cat did a flip.

16. Jill had to fill the bucket. It spilled.

FITNESS FLASH: Lie on your stomach, lift your arms and legs off the floor, and pretend to swim. Do this three times for 10 seconds each.

109

109

Answer Key

The sentence below uses all letters of the alphabet. Use it to practice your handwriting.

A dozen brave ex-knights will quest for juicy plums.

A dozen
brave ex-knights
will quest for
juicy plums.

110

Read the poem. Underline all the words that have the short i sound. Then, answer the questions.

Big Hit

At the farm shindig*, there's a pig in a wig
Who is dancing a jig—I'm not lying.
Now, her twin starts to spin on the floor with a grin,
But she steps on a pin and goes flying.

In the air, she does flips as she snacks on some chips
That she had in her lips the whole time.
The first sis is in bliss* as she sees all of this.
See, her twin's found a new way to dine!

*shindig *n.* party
*bliss *n.* great happiness

1. How many pigs are talked about in the poem?
   a. two
   b. three
   c. four

2. What happens to make one of the pigs fly into the air?
   a. She snacks on some chips.
   b. She spins on the floor.
   c. She steps on a pin.

3. What is a jig?
   a. a kind of dance
   b. a kind of snack
   c. a kind of toy

FACTOID: Pigs are very smart, maybe even smarter than a three-year-old child.

112

BONUS

City Streets

Every town has some interesting street names. Streets can get their names in many different ways. They are often named after presidents, states, trees, and flowers. What are some of the interesting street names in your town?

People's Names	Places	Funny Names
Numbers	Natural Features	Animals
Plants and Trees	Directions	Other

Answers will vary.

113

Say the name of each picture. Write o to complete each word that has the short o sound heard in frog.

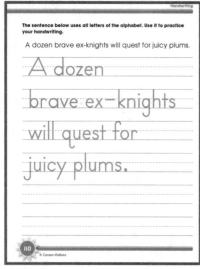

1. f o x
2. cl o ck
3. l o ck
4. b o g
5. v o n
6. s o ck

115

Use the calendar to answer each question.

July

Sunday	Monday	Tuesday	Wednesday	Thursday	Friday	Saturday
		1	2	3	4	5
6	7	8	9	10	11	12
13	14	15	16	17	18	19
20	21	22	23	24	25	26
27	28	29	30	31		

1. What day of the week is July 14? Monday
2. What day of the week is the first day of July? Tuesday
3. What date is the second Wednesday? July 9
4. What day of the week is July 31? Thursday

CHARACTER CHECK: What is one mistake you made recently? What did you learn from that mistake?

116

In each row, circle the three objects that most belong together.

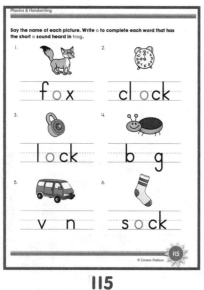

117

Answer Key

Add or subtract to solve each probem. Use the 10 dots below to help you solve.

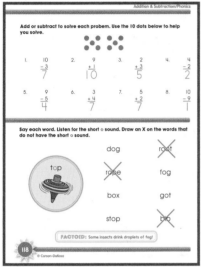

1. 10 − 3 = 7	2. 9 + 1 = 10	3. 2 + 3 = 5	4. 4 − 2 = 2
5. 9 − 5 = 4	6. 3 + 4 = 7	7. 5 + 2 = 7	8. 10 − 9 = 1

Say each word. Listen for the short o sound. Draw an X on the words that do not have the short o sound.

top

dog   ~~root~~

~~rope~~   fog

box   got

stop   ~~big~~

FACTOID: Some insects drink droplets of fog!

118

Look at the picture below. Circle the things that go fast. Draw an X on each thing that is slow.

119

Look at the picture graph.

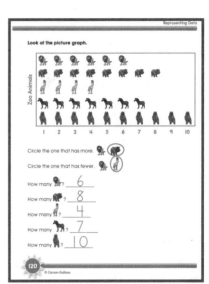

Circle the one that has more.

Circle the one that has fewer.

How many 🐘? 6

How many 🦁? 8

How many 🐴? 4

How many 🐴? 7

How many 🐻? 10

120

Add or subtract to solve each problem.

1. 6 + 2 = 8
2. 5 − 1 = 4
3. 4 + 3 = 7
4. 8 − 1 = 7
5. 2 + 8 = 10
6. 9 − 0 = 9
7. 3 + 5 = 8
8. 10 − 6 = 4
9. 7 + 2 = 9
10. 9 − 8 = 1
11. 1 + 9 = 10
12. 6 − 3 = 3

Read each sentence aloud. Listen for the short o sound. Circle each word that has the short o sound.

13. The (frog) can (hop) on (top) of the (box).
14. The (dog) and the (fox) ran to the (pond).
15. (John) put the (box) by the (rock).
16. (Tom) went for a (jog).

FITNESS FLASH: Bear-walk across the room and back.

121

Make a food chart for one day. Show what you ate.

Fruit Vegetable Meat/Eggs/Fish Bread/Cereal Other Foods

Breakfast	
Lunch	Answers will vary.
Dinner	
Snacks	

Use your food chart.

1. How many of each did you eat?

Fruit _____   Bread/Cereal _____

Vegetable _____   Other Foods _____

Meat/Eggs Answers will vary.

2. What food did you eat the most? _____
3. At which meal did you eat the most? _____
4. What is your favorite food? _____

122

Follow the directions to draw a picture.

1. Draw 1 ● in the middle of the pig's face to make a nose.
2. Draw 2 ● inside the nose to finish it.
3. Draw 1 ⌣ underneath the nose to make a mouth.
4. Draw 2 ● above the nose to make eyes.
5. Draw 2 ◁ on either side of the head to make ears.

123

Answer Key

124

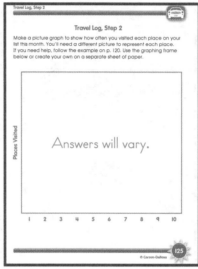

125

126

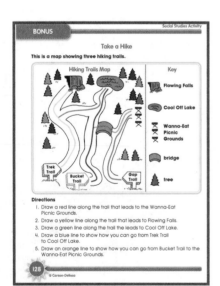

128

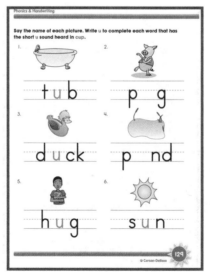

129

130

Answer Key

Follow the clues below. Circle your choices.

1. Find the object that is brown and **hard**.

2. Find the object that is yellow and **long**.

3. Find the object that is **green** and **sour**.

4. Find the object that is **blue** and tiny.

131

Write the missing numbers in each fact family.

1. Family: 2, 3, 5

$3 + \boxed{2} = 5$

$2 + 3 = \boxed{5}$

$5 - \boxed{3} = 2$

$5 - 2 = \boxed{3}$

2. Family: 3, 1, 4

$1 + \boxed{3} = 4$

$3 + 1 = \boxed{4}$

$4 - 3 = \boxed{1}$

$4 - \boxed{3} = 1$

Say each word. Listen for the short u sound. Draw an X on the words that do not have the short u sound.

rug

b̶o̶o̶k̶   fun

dug   h̶a̶t̶

c̶u̶b̶e̶   us

up   shut

FACTOID: Reading storybooks can make you better at understanding how other people feel.

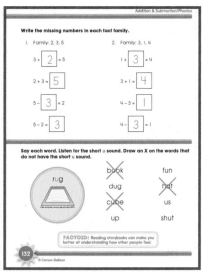

132

Circle the picture that is most different in each row.

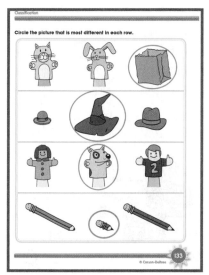

133

Follow the directions to draw a picture.

1. Draw 1 ● in the center of the page to make a body.

2. Draw 1 ● on top of the big circle to make a head.

3. Draw 8 ∧ around the big circle to make legs.

4. Draw 2 o in the small circle to make eyes.

134

Write the missing numbers in each fact family.

1. Family: 3, 6, 9

$6 + \boxed{3} = 9$

$3 + 6 = \boxed{9}$

$9 - \boxed{6} = 3$

$9 - 3 = \boxed{6}$

2. Family: 2, 5, 7

$5 + \boxed{2} = 7$

$2 + 5 = \boxed{7}$

$7 - 2 = \boxed{5}$

$7 - \boxed{2} = 5$

Read each sentence aloud. Listen for the short u sound. Circle each word that has the short u sound.

3. The (lucky) (duck) swam on the pond.

4. Mom (cut) the (bud) off the (shrub).

5. (Gus) chewed (gum) on the (bus).

6. (Judd) washed the (mud) out of the (rug).

CHARACTER CHECK: Be brave and try something new this week.

135

Circle the numbers that match the first number in each row.

25	(25)	52	20	(25)	22	55	(25)	26
98	96	89	(98)	93	88	(98)	99	(98)
16	10	61	18	(16)	26	(16)	67	(16)

Color each word the correct color. Then, write the word on the line.

red   red

blue   blue

yellow   yellow

green   green

136

Answer Key

Nouns can name things.

car

ball

Fill in the missing letters in the nouns that name things. Use the words in the box to help you.

chair   desk   book   apple   pen   bag

bag   book   apple

desk

pen

chair

137

Read the poem. Underline all the words that have the short u sound. Then, answer the questions.

Get Up, Pup!

Each day after <u>lunch</u> at about <u>one</u> o'clock
<u>Chuck</u> has little <u>luck</u> getting his <u>pup</u> to wake <u>up</u>.

He calls his <u>pup</u>'s name and lets in the <u>sun</u>
<u>But</u> for that <u>pup</u> to get <u>up</u>, <u>Chuck</u> <u>must</u> beat a <u>drum</u>!

The <u>pup</u> <u>does</u> not like this—it is not at all <u>fun</u>—
He drags himself <u>up</u>, <u>but</u> his eyes are still <u>shut</u>!

So <u>Chuck</u> gives him a <u>hug</u> and a <u>muffin</u> with <u>nuts</u>,
The <u>pup</u> opens his eyes and, at last, he says, "<u>Ruff</u>!"

1. What problem does Chuck have?
   a. His pup is late for lunch.
   (b) His pup will not wake up.
   c. His pup does not like drums.

2. How do we know when the pup is really awake?
   a. He beats a drum.
   b. He gets out of bed.
   (c) He opens his eyes and barks.

3. Which sentence best describes Chuck?
   (a) Chuck cares about his pup.
   b. Chuck is angry with his pup.
   c. Chuck wants his pup to play drums.

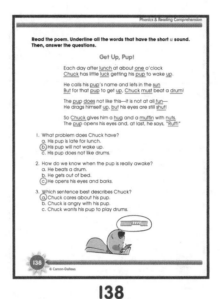

138

Travel Log, Final Step

On page 93, you practiced writing an opinion. When you write an advertisement, or ad, your goal is to get people to have a good opinion about whatever it is you're advertising. Since you chose for your ad a place you like to go, your goal here is to make other people want to go there, too.

Directions
1. Choose the place you liked best from your graph on page 125.
2. Fill in the worksheet below to get ready to write your ad.
3. Look at the example on page 140 to get writing ideas.
4. Write your own ad on a separate sheet of paper.
5. Perform your ad for an audience. Think about recording it so that you can play it like an ad on the radio.

What is the name of your chosen place? _____

What can people do there? _____

What did yc   Answers will vary. ———

What do you think other people will like the most about this place?
_____
_____

What sound effects could you use in your ad? Start by thinking about what sounds you heard when you visited the place you're advertising.
_____
_____
_____

139

BONUS

Heroes

Who is your hero?
Answer the questions.
Draw a picture of this
person in the box.

Name: _____

What do you like about this person?

———   Answers will vary. ———

What would you like to do with this person?
_____
_____
_____
_____

144

ABC Book of Summer Adventures, Step 1

Do something fun for every letter of the alphabet! In this exploration, you will take or draw pictures of your summer adventures. Then, you will turn those adventures into an ABC book!

To begin, make a list of your favorite things to do in the summer. Maybe you like making popsicles with your parents, playing baseball with friends, or going swimming at the lake. Include any favorite things you have done so far plus anything you would like to do before you go back to school. Continue on a separate sheet of paper, if needed.

FAVORITE SUMMER ACTIVITIES

1. _____
2. _____
3. _____
4. _____
5. _____
6. ——— Answers will vary. ———
7. _____
8. _____
9. _____
10. _____
11. _____
12. _____

147

Summer Fun Puppet Show, Step 1

Before going back to school, relive the summer! In this exploration, you will turn your favorite summer adventures into a puppet show!

To begin, think about all the fun things you have done this summer. Did you travel anywhere? Did you have a particularly fun day at the park? Did you sleep over at a friend's house? Make a list of your adventures. Is there anything else you would like to do before back-to-school? Put those on the list, too, and see if you can make them happen. Continue on a separate sheet of paper, if needed.

SUMMER ADVENTURES

1. _____
2. _____
3. _____
4. _____
5. _____
6. ——— Answers will vary. ———
7. _____
8. _____
9. _____
10. _____
11. _____
12. _____

148

Answer Key

149

Addition/ABC Order

Add to find each sum.

1. 6 + 2 = 8   2. 5 + 1 = 6   3. 4 + 3 = 7

4. 1 + 7 = 8   5. 2 + 8 = 10   6. 9 + 0 = 9

7. 3 + 5 = 8   8. 4 + 6 = 10   9. 7 + 2 = 9

Circle the first letter of each word below. Then, put the words in ABC order. The first one is done for you.

10. car bird — **bird** / car
11. moon two — moon / two
12. nest fan — fan / nest

13. card dog — card / dog
14. pig bike — bike / pig
15. sun pie — pie / sun

149

150

Phonics & Handwriting

Write the beginning sound for each picture.

1. d   2. m   3. c   4. s

5. c   6. b   7. t   8. d

9. m   10. t   11. s   12. b

150

151

Subtraction/ABC Order

Subtract to find each difference.

1. 6 − 2 = 4   2. 5 − 1 = 4   3. 7 − 3 = 4

4. 8 − 7 = 1   5. 10 − 8 = 2   6. 9 − 0 = 9

7. 8 − 4 = 4   8. 10 − 6 = 4   9. 7 − 2 = 5

10. 9 − 1 = 8   11. 6 − 3 = 3   12. 10 − 4 = 6

Put each row of words in ABC order. If the first letters of two words are the same, look at the second or third letters.

13. 1 candy   2 carrot   4 duck   3 dance

14. 2 cold   4 hot   1 carry   3 hit

15. 2 flash   1 fan   3 fun   4 garden

16. 2 seat   4 sun   1 saw   3 sit

151

152

Addition & Subtraction

Add or subtract to solve each problem.

1. 9 − 3 = 6   2. 6 + 4 = 10   3. 5 + 3 = 8

4. 2 + 7 = 9   5. 8 − 2 = 6   6. 7 − 5 = 2

7. 4 + 5 = 9   8. 6 − 3 = 3   9. 6 + 3 = 9

10. 8 − 3 = 5   11. 9 − 4 = 5   12. 9 − 5 = 4

13. 5 + 4 = 9   14. 4 − 3 = 1   15. 7 + 2 = 9

CHARACTER CHECK: What is your best skill? What can you do to get even better at it?

152

153

ABC Book of Summer Adventures, Step 2

ABC

ABC Book of Summer Adventures, Step 2

Keep track of the fun things you do this month. Each time you do one of your favorite things, take a picture or draw something to represent your adventure. Then, on this sheet, write a brief description of what you did. Continue on a separate sheet of paper. Also, if you would like, check items off your list of favorites on page 147 as you go.

1.
2.
3.
4.
5.
6. Answers will vary.
7.
8.
9.
10.

153

154

Phonics/Grammar & Handwriting

Say the name of each picture. Draw a line to the letter that makes the same vowel sound.

a   e   i   o   u

Write each noun next to the correct box.

girl   truck   zoo
school   ball   baby

Person — girl   baby
Place — school   zoo
Thing — truck   ball

154

237

© Carson-Dellosa

Answer Key

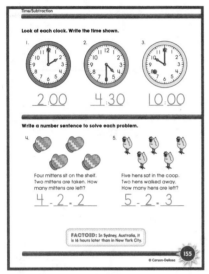

Look at each clock. Write the time shown.

1. 2:00
2. 4:30
3. 10:00

Write a number sentence to solve each problem.

4. Four mittens sit on the shelf. Two mittens are taken. How many mittens are left?
4 - 2 = 2

5. Five hens sat in the coop. Two hens walked away. How many hens are left?
5 - 2 = 3

FACTOID: In Sydney, Australia, it is 16 hours later than in New York City.

155

155

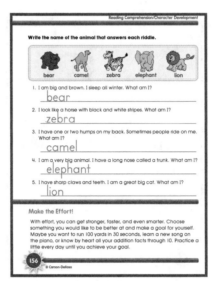

Write the name of the animal that answers each riddle.

bear   camel   zebra   elephant   lion

1. I am big and brown. I sleep all winter. What am I?
bear

2. I look like a horse with black and white stripes. What am I?
zebra

3. I have one or two humps on my back. Sometimes people ride on me. What am I?
camel

4. I am a very big animal. I have a long nose called a trunk. What am I?
elephant

5. I have sharp claws and teeth. I am a great big cat. What am I?
lion

Make the Effort!

With effort, you can get stronger, faster, and even smarter. Choose something you would like to be better at and make a goal for yourself. Maybe you want to run 100 yards in 30 seconds, learn a new song on the piano, or know by heart all your addition facts through 10. Practice a little every day until you achieve your goal.

156

156

Write a, e, i, o, or u on each line.

p i g   c a t   b a t

h e n   fr o g   d u ck

When you count pennies, you count by 1s. Count each set of pennies. Write the amount on each jar.

1. 4¢
2. 7¢

157

157

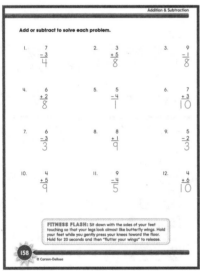

Add or subtract to solve each problem.

1. 7 - 3 = 4
2. 3 + 5 = 8
3. 9 - 1 = 8
4. 6 + 2 = 8
5. 5 - 4 = 1
6. 7 + 3 = 10
7. 6 - 3 = 3
8. 8 + 1 = 9
9. 5 - 2 = 3
10. 4 + 5 = 9
11. 9 - 4 = 5
12. 4 + 6 = 10

FITNESS FLASH: Sit down with the soles of your feet touching so that your legs look almost like butterfly wings. Hold your feet while you gently press your knees toward the floor. Hold for 20 seconds and then "flutter your wings" to release.

158

158

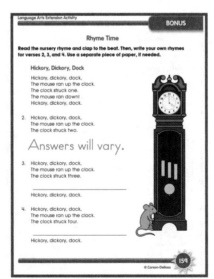

BONUS

Rhyme Time

Read the nursery rhyme and clap to the beat. Then, write your own rhymes for verses 2, 3, and 4. Use a separate piece of paper, if needed.

Hickory, Dickory, Dock

Hickory, dickory, dock,
The mouse ran up the clock.
The clock struck one.
The mouse ran down!
Hickory, dickory, dock.

2. Hickory, dickory, dock,
The mouse ran up the clock.
The clock struck two.

Answers will vary.

3. Hickory, dickory, dock,
The mouse ran up the clock.
The clock struck three.

Hickory, dickory, dock.

4. Hickory, dickory, dock,
The mouse ran up the clock.
The clock struck four.

Hickory, dickory, dock.

159

159

Circle the pairs that rhyme.

1. map   nest
2. dog   frog
3. hat   bat
4. kite   mop
5. can   fan
6. rat   pig

161

161

Answer Key

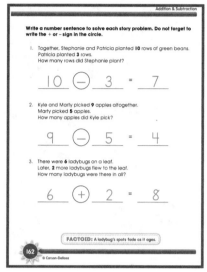

162

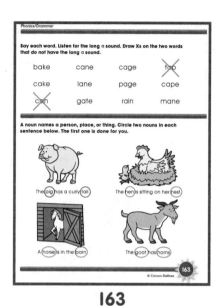

163

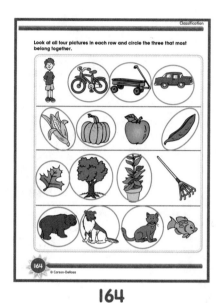

164

Addition & Subtraction/Counting & Money

Add or subtract to solve each problem.

1. 9 − 3 = **6**   2. 6 + 4 = **10**   3. 5 + 3 = **8**
4. 2 + 7 = **9**   5. 8 − 2 = **6**   6. 7 − 5 = **2**
7. 4 + 5 = **9**   8. 6 − 3 = **3**   9. 6 + 3 = **9**
10. 8 − 3 = **5**   11. 9 − 4 = **5**   12. 9 − 5 = **4**
13. 5 + 4 = **9**   14. 4 − 3 = **1**   15. 7 + 2 = **9**

When you count nickels, you count by 5s. Count each set of nickels. Write the total amount.

16. 5¢ 5¢ 5¢ 5¢ **20**¢   17. 5¢ 5¢ **10**¢
18. 5¢ 5¢ 5¢ **15**¢   19. 5¢ 5¢ 5¢ 5¢ 5¢ **25**¢

165

Phonics

Say the name of each picture. Write the letters you hear to spell each word.

1. c a k e
2. t a p e
3. v a s e
4. n a i l
5. r a i n
6. p a i n t

REMINDER: Have you made any last adventures happen this month? Take another look at the list you started on page 148. See if you can do at least one more fun thing on your list before the summer is over.

166

Addition & Subtraction/Time

Write the missing numbers in each fact family.

1. Family: 4, 5, 9
   5 + **4** = 9
   4 + 5 = **9**
   9 − **5** = 4
   9 − 4 = **5**

2. Family: 2, 8, 10
   8 + **2** = 10
   2 + 8 = **10**
   10 − 2 = **8**
   10 − **2** = 8

Look at each clock. Write the time shown.

3. **7:00**   4. **5:30**   5. **1:00**

FACTOID: In very hot and dry places, rain can evaporate before it hits the ground!

167

Answer Key

Draw a line from the sign to the sentence that tells about it.

1. If you see this sign, watch out for trains.

2. When cars or bikes come to this sign, they must stop.

3. When this sign is on, do not cross the street.

4. This sign tells you to stay out of the yard.

5. If you see this sign, do not eat or drink what is inside!

6. This sign warns you that it is not safe. Stay away!

7. This sign says you are not allowed to come in.

168

Say each word. Listen for the long e sound. Draw Xs on the two words that do not have the long e sound.

eel	queen	feet	~~rose~~
feel	seed	sweet	beak
pea	bead	~~red~~	beach

Dad and Ana are cooking. Circle the action word in each sentence that tells what they do.

1. Dad (chops).
2. Ana (mixes).
3. Ana (stirs).
4. Ana (washes).
5. Dad (peels).
6. They (bake).

CHARACTER CHECK: Think about how you can help your classmates next year. What can you teach others?

169

Circle one picture that most belongs with the first picture in each row.

170

BONUS

Subtraction Color Code

Subtract to solve each problem. Then, use the code to color the spaces.

Color Code:
0 = green   1 = brown   2 = blue   3 = purple   4 = black   5 = pink

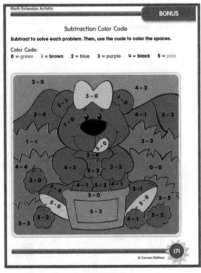

171

BONUS

Tell Me More!

Find out what your friend loves more than anything in the world. Learn about what your family did before you were born. Discover your neighbor's greatest achievement. Practice your questioning skills and find out more!

Step 1: Think of someone you want to know more about. This should be a friend, family member, or neighbor you know and trust.

Step 2: Think of something you would like to know about that person. What are you curious about?

Step 3: Using the question words below, write at least one of each type of question. Work hard to make your questions about what you really want to find out.

Step 4: Set up your interview and ask away! Remember what you find out and share it with a friend or family member. You may also want to draw a picture of the person you interviewed.

Who _____?
What _____?
Where ____ Answers will vary. ____?
When _____?
Why _____?

172

Say the name of each picture. Write the letter of the beginning sound.

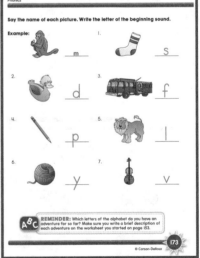

Example: m

1. s
2. d
3. f
4. p
5. l
6. y
7. v

REMINDER: Which letters of the alphabet do you have an adventure for so far? Make sure you write a brief description of each adventure on the worksheet you started on page 153.

173

Answer Key

174

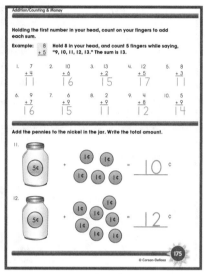

175

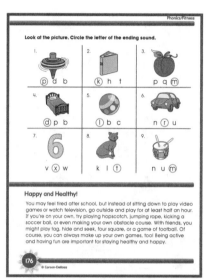

176

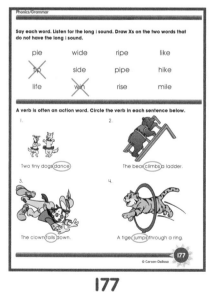

177

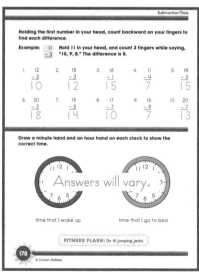

178

Page 179

179

Answer Key

Say the name of each picture. Write the letters you hear to spell each word.

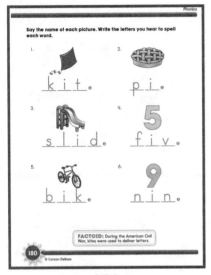

1. k i t e
2. p i e
3. s l i d e
4. f i v e
5. b i k e
6. n i n e

FACTOID: During the American Civil War, kites were used to deliver letters.

180

Add or subtract to solve each problem.

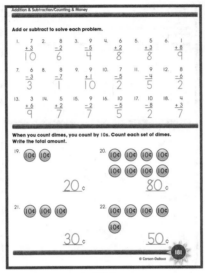

1. 7 +3 = 10	2. 8 −2 = 6	3. 9 −5 = 4	4. 6 +2 = 8	5. 5 +3 = 8	6. 1 +8 = 9
7. 6 −3 = 3	8. 8 −7 = 1	9. 9 +1 = 10	10. 7 −5 = 2	11. 9 −4 = 5	12. 8 −6 = 2
13. 3 +6 = 9	14. 5 +2 = 7	15. 9 −2 = 7	16. 10 −5 = 5	17. 10 −8 = 2	18. 4 +3 = 7

When you count dimes, you count by 10s. Count each set of dimes. Write the total amount.

19. 10¢ 10¢ = 20¢
20. 10¢ 10¢ 10¢ 10¢ / 10¢ 10¢ 10¢ 10¢ = 80¢
21. 10¢ 10¢ 10¢ = 30¢
22. 10¢ 10¢ 10¢ 10¢ / 10¢ = 50¢

181

Say the name of each picture. Write the correct beginning and ending sounds.

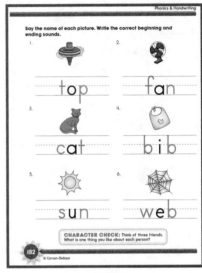

1. top
2. fan
3. cat
4. bib
5. sun
6. web

CHARACTER CHECK: Think of three friends. What is one thing you like about each person?

182

BONUS

Choose a New Ending!

Look at the picture story below.

Imagine a new ending to the story. Draw your ending in the box.

Answers will vary.

183

BONUS

Grasping Objects

How do your thumbs help you grasp objects?

Materials
- tape
- pencil
- several small objects

Procedure
Have an adult help you tape the thumb of your writing hand to your palm so that you cannot move it. The tape should allow your other fingers to move freely. Try to pick up a pencil and write your name. Then, try to tie your shoes. Next, try to pick up each small object.

Remove the tape. Repeat each activity. Notice how your thumb works as you complete each activity.

1. Circle the activity that was easier.
   A. writing with a taped hand
   (B) writing with no tape on your hand

2. Circle the activity that was more difficult.
   A. tying your shoe with no tape on your hand
   (B) tying your shoe with a taped hand

3. Circle the names of the animals who have thumbs that help them grasp objects.
   (monkey) fish
   frog (gorilla)

184

Say each word. Listen for the long o sound. Draw Xs on the two words that do not have the long o sound.

hose	note	joke	bone
rose	pa~~ge~~	poke	p~~ad~~
toad	boat	roast	goat

A preposition can show where something is or which way it is going. Circle the preposition that matches each picture.

Dax passed the ball **from/(to)** Ella.

The cat is **(under)/next to** the desk.

The balloon is **after/(above)** the girl.

185

Answer Key

Holding the first number in your head, count on your fingers to add each sum.

Example: 6 Hold 6 in your head, and count 6 fingers while saying,
         +6 "7, 8, 9, 10, 11, 12." The sum is 12.

1. 8   2. 10   3. 9   4. 12   5. 8
   +4   +3   +2   +7   +8
   12   13   11   19   16

6. 11   7. 11   8. 13   9. 4   10. 16
   +7   +9   +6   +9   +4
   18   18   19   13   20

Circle the picture that rhymes with the first picture in each row.

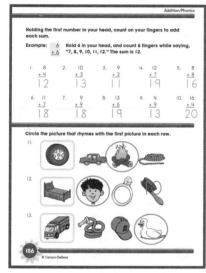

© Carson-Dellosa

186

Say the name of each picture. Write the letters you hear to spell each word.

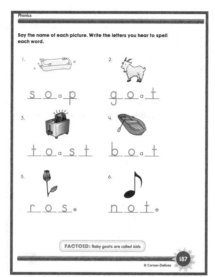

1. s o a p   2. g o a t
3. t o a s t   4. b o a t
5. r o s e   6. n o t e

FACTOID: Baby goats are called *kids*.

© Carson-Dellosa

187

Holding the first number in your head, count backward on your fingers to find each difference.

Example: 14 Hold 14 in your head, and count 5 fingers while saying,
         −5   "13, 12, 11, 10, 9." The difference is 9.

1. 16   2. 13   3. 16   4. 11   5. 17
   −2   −4   −6   −3   −5
   14   9   10   8   12

6. 19   7. 20   8. 17   9. 18   10. 20
   −6   −5   −4   −9   −10
   13   15   13   9   10

Fill in the blank with a word that rhymes with the underlined word.

11.
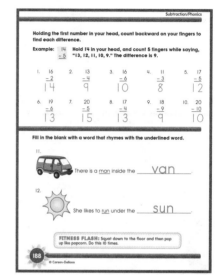
There is a man inside the ___van___.

12.
She likes to run under the ___sun___.

FITNESS FLASH: Squat down to the floor and then pop up like popcorn. Do this 10 times.

© Carson-Dellosa

188

ABC Book of Summer Adventures, Step 3

Make sure you have one summer activity for each letter of the alphabet. You may need to get creative with names for things. For example, for the letter X, maybe you list an "Extra Special Shopping Trip" or an "Exciting Day at the Beach." Write the name for each activity on the chart or on a separate sheet of paper if you need more room.

A	N
B	O
C	P
D	Q
E	R
F	
G	Answers will vary.
H	U
I	V
J	W
K	X
L	Y
M	Z

© Carson-Dellosa

189

Summer Fun Puppet Show, Step 2

Return to your list of summer adventures on page 148. Cross off anything that did not happen this summer. Then, choose your three favorite adventures to turn into a puppet show. Who are the most important people in those adventures? They will become the puppets in your show. Make sure to include yourself and at least one other person.

Adventure 1:
What happened? _____

Most important people? _____

Adventure : Answers will vary.
What happ-

Most important people? _____

Adventure 3:
What happened? _____

Most important people? _____

© Carson-Dellosa

190

Lincoln counted the number of black, white, red, and green cars he saw on the way to the grocery store with his dad. He then drew a car for each one he saw. Color the graph to show how many cars of each color Lincoln saw.

Cars on the Road

Lincoln saw fewer ___green___ cars than any other color.

© Carson-Dellosa

191

Answer Key

Solve for the missing number in each equation. Write the number in the box.

1. 6 +[4] =10	2. 3 +[5] =8	3. [5] +4 =9	4. [2] +5 =7
5. 8 +[1] =9	6. 7 +[3] =10	7. [6] +2 =8	8. [5] +5 =10

Write what makes you happy. Write what makes you sad.

_____

_____ makes me happy.

Answers will vary.

_____ makes me sad.

192

Say each word. Listen for the long u sound. Draw Xs on the two words that do not have the long u sound.

cute	tune	fume	music
~~two~~	mule	fuse	cube
~~up~~	mute	tube	juice

Choose a preposition to complete each sentence. Write it on the line.

off	into	in

Ling hid ___in___ the shed.

at	on	up

The cat can jump ___on___ the table.

193

Solve for the missing number in each equation. Write the number in the box.

1. 9 -[6] =3	2. 10 -[3] =7	3. [8] -4 =4	4. [9] -7 =2
5. 10 -[9] =1	6. 7 -[4] =3	7. [7] -5 =2	8. [10] -10 =0

Use the letters in the box to see how many words can you make. You will use each letter more than once.

b   Answers will vary.   t

p an	p at	t in
m an	r at	p in
r an	b at	b ug
t an	s at	t ug
b ut	b et	p op
p ut	p et	m op

194

Table Fort

Read the story. Then, answer the questions.

"Mom, can we build a fort in the dining room?" John asked.

"Sure, Honey," said John's mom. Then, the two found a giant sheet and covered the dining room table with it.

The fort was built! The only problem was the door to the fort would not stay shut. John tried putting pillows on top, but the sheet kept slipping open.

John's mom said, "We need something stronger to hold these ends together."

"I'll be right back!" said John, and he ran to the laundry room. He came back with three clothespins. John and his mom used them to clip the ends of the sheet together.

"Yes! It worked!" said John. "Let's eat lunch inside the fort!"

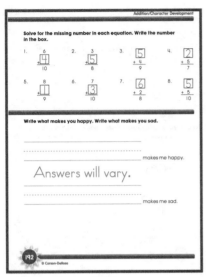

1. What problem did John and his mom have?
a. John wanted to build a fort, but his mom did not.
b. The dining room table was covered in pillows.
c.) The door to the fort would not stay closed.

2. How was the problem solved?
a.) John found clothespins to clip the sheet's ends together.
b. John begged his mom to let him build a fort.
c. John helped his mom put the pillows away.

3. Which sentence best describes John and his mom?
a.) They work well together.
b. They do not agree.
c. They do not like messes.

FITNESS FLASH: Do a silly dance for 60 seconds. See how fast you can move your arms and legs!

195

Say the name of each picture. Write the letter sounds you hear to spell each word.

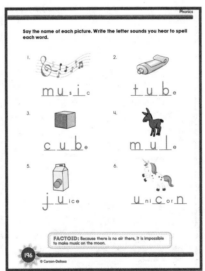

1. mu s i c

2. t u b e

3. c u b e

4. m u l e

5. j u ice

6. u ni c o r n

FACTOID: Because there is no air there, it is impossible to make music on the moon.

196

Moon Code

Max is pretending to fly through the solar system. He wants to visit more moons.

Use the code to discover the names of some moons in our solar system.

A	B	C	D	E	F	G	H	I	J	K	L	M
1	2	3	4	5	6	7	8	9	10	11	12	13

N	O	P	Q	R	S	T	U	V	W	X	Y	Z
14	15	16	17	18	19	20	21	22	23	24	25	26

First, he sees Jupiter's moon named I o. It has at least eight active volcanoes.
  9 15

P h o b o s travels around Mars in 7½ hours. No other moon
16 8 15 2 15 19

travels so fast!

Next, he goes to the largest moon in the solar system.

It is named G a n y m e d e. It orbits Jupiter.
  7 1 14 25 13 5 4 5

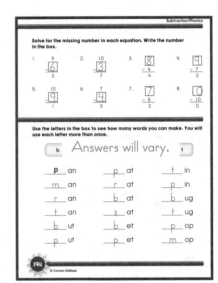

197

© Carson-Dellosa

Answer Key

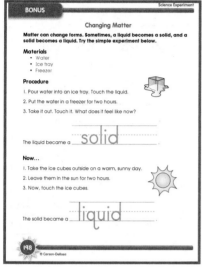

198

Changing Matter

Matter can change forms. Sometimes, a liquid becomes a solid, and a solid becomes a liquid. Try the simple experiment below.

Materials
- Water
- Ice tray
- Freezer

Procedure
1. Pour water into an ice tray. Touch the liquid.
2. Put the water in a freezer for two hours.
3. Take it out. Touch it. What does it feel like now?

The liquid became a **solid**

Now...
1. Take the ice cubes outside on a warm, sunny day.
2. Leave them in the sun for two hours.
3. Now, touch the ice cubes.

The solid became a **liquid**

198

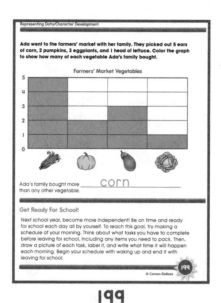

199

Representing Data/Character Development

Ada went to the farmers' market with her family. They picked out 5 ears of corn, 2 pumpkins, 3 eggplants, and 1 head of lettuce. Color the graph to show how many of each vegetable Ada's family bought.

Farmers' Market Vegetables

Ada's family bought more than any other vegetable. **corn**

Get Ready For School!

Next school year, become more independent! Be on time and ready for school each day all by yourself. To reach this goal, try making a schedule of your morning. Think about what tasks you have to complete before leaving for school, including any items you need to pack. Then, draw a picture of each task, label it, and write what time it will happen each morning. Begin your schedule with waking up and end it with leaving for school.

199

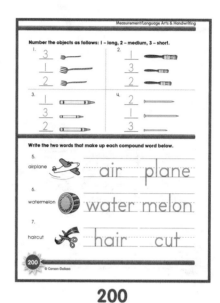

200

Measurement/Language Arts & Handwriting

Number the objects as follows: 1 – long, 2 – medium, 3 – short.

1.   3 / 1 / 2
2.   1 / 3 / 2
3.   1 / 3 / 2
4.   2 / 1 / 3

Write the two words that make up each compound word below.

5. airplane — **air** **plane**

6. watermelon — **water** **melon**

7. haircut — **hair** **cut**

200

201

Addition & Subtraction/Phonics

Add or subtract to solve each problem.

1. 5 + 2 = **7**
2. 9 – 3 = **6**
3. 9 + 1 = **10**
4. 7 – 4 = **3**
5. 6 + 2 = **8**
6. 8 – 5 = **3**
7. 4 + 5 = **9**
8. 10 – 2 = **8**
9. 7 + 3 = **10**
10. 8 – 4 = **4**
11. 5 + 5 = **10**
12. 6 – 3 = **3**
13. 10 + 0 = **10**
14. 6 – 4 = **2**
15. 5 + 3 = **8**

Say the name of each picture. Circle the number that tells how many syllables are in each name.

16. 1 (2)
17. (1) 2
18. 1 (2)

CHARACTER CHECK: Make an effort to say hello to your classmates on the first day of school, even the ones you don't know.

201

202

Measurement/Language Arts & Handwriting

Use the paper clips to measure each object.

1. **3** paper clips
2. **5** paper clips

Underline the two words in each sentence that can make a compound word. Write the compound word on the line to complete the sentence.

3. A kind of <u>bird</u> that is <u>black</u> is a **blackbird**

4. A <u>horse</u> that can <u>race</u> is a **racehorse**

5. A <u>cloth</u> that covers a <u>table</u> is a **tablecloth**

202

203

Addition & Subtraction/Numbers

Add or subtract to solve each probem.

1. 2 + 3 = **5**
2. 4 + 4 = **8**
3. 5 + 2 = **7**
4. 6 + 3 = **9**
5. 3 + 4 = **7**
6. 4 – 1 = **3**
7. 8 – 6 = **2**
8. 9 – 5 = **4**
9. 6 – 2 = **4**
10. 7 – 6 = **1**

Write the missing numbers.

1	2	3	4	5	6	7	8	9	10
11	12	13	14	15	16	17	18	19	20
21	22	23	24	25	26	27	28	29	30
31	32	33	34	35	36	37	38	39	40
41	42	43	44	45	46	47	48	49	50
51	52	53	54	55	56	57	58	59	60

203

Answer Key

Color the kittens using the clues below.

The first kitten wears silver bracelets and purple boots. It is pushing on the ball of green yarn.

The second kitten is lounging on top of the ball of green yarn. It is wearing a blue T-shirt.

The third kitten wears a red top hat. It is pulling on the ball of green yarn.

FITNESS FLASH: Lie on your back with your legs straight. Lift both legs at the same time and slowly lower them until they are almost touching the floor. Hold for 10 seconds.

206

Add or subtract to solve each problem. Use the ten frames for help.

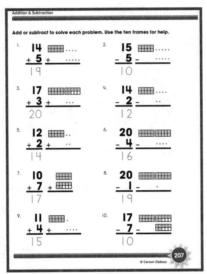

1. $14 + 5 = 19$
2. $15 - 5 = 10$
3. $17 + 3 = 20$
4. $14 - 2 = 12$
5. $12 + 2 = 14$
6. $20 - 4 = 16$
7. $10 + 7 = 17$
8. $20 - 1 = 19$
9. $11 + 4 = 15$
10. $17 - 7 = 10$

207

Draw lines between pictures that rhyme.

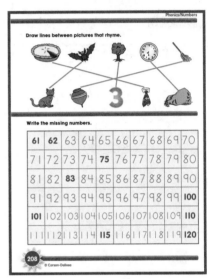

Write the missing numbers.

61	62	63	64	65	66	67	68	69	70
71	72	73	74	75	76	77	78	79	80
81	82	83	84	85	86	87	88	89	90
91	92	93	94	95	96	97	98	99	100
101	102	103	104	105	106	107	108	109	110
111	112	113	114	115	116	117	118	119	120

208

Read the passage. Then, answer the questions.

Penguins

Penguins are birds, but they cannot fly. Instead, penguins are very good swimmers and spend a lot of time in the water. Their wings help them swim! Penguins' wings are really more like flippers, which they flap to swim. Most penguins can swim up to 7 miles per hour. Some penguins can swim as fast as 22 miles per hour! Other animals in the water hunt penguins, so penguins need to be extra fast. Penguins' white belly feathers and black back feathers make it hard for other animals to spot them. This helps keep penguins safe.

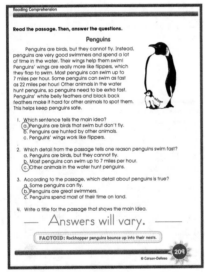

1. Which sentence tells the main idea?
   a. Penguins are birds that swim but don't fly.
   b. Penguins are hunted by other animals.
   c. Penguins' wings work like flippers.

2. Which detail from the passage tells one reason penguins swim fast?
   a. Penguins are birds, but they cannot fly.
   b. Most penguins can swim up to 7 miles per hour.
   c. Other animals in the water hunt penguins.

3. According to the passage, which detail about penguins is true?
   a. Some penguins can fly.
   b. Penguins are great swimmers.
   c. Penguins spend most of their time on land.

4. Write a title for the passage that shows the main idea.
   — Answers will vary. —

FACTOID: Rockhopper penguins bounce up into their nests.

209

Write your name. Make each letter into a picture.

JASON

Pictures will vary.

210

First-Grade Goals

Make sure you have the best possible year in first grade! Set goals for the new school year and work toward achieving them.

What skills would you like to make progress in by the end of the year? Are you shy about asking questions? If so, set a goal to ask at least one question per day. Do you love to read? Set a reading goal. How many books can you read each week? Maybe you have a hard time staying organized. A good goal might be to clear out your backpack every night before bed.

List your first-grade goals here. Then, check back during the school year to track your success! As you meet your goal each month, put a checkmark in one of the small boxes. At the end of the year, you can draw a star in the big box to show you met your goal for the school year.

Goal 1 _____

| 1 | 2 | 3 | 4 | 5 | 6 | 7 | 8 | 9 | |

Answers will vary.

Goal 2 _____

| 1 | 2 | 3 | 4 | 5 | 6 | 7 | 8 | 9 | |

Goal 3 _____

| 1 | 2 | 3 | 4 | 5 | 6 | 7 | 8 | 9 | |

216